AF593758

# The Definitive Book of The Tarot

# The Definitive Book of The Tarot

Kathleen McCormack

First published in Great Britain by
David Westnedge Ltd.


The IJJ Tarot Cards used on the cover are reproduced
by kind permission of A. G. Müller, Switzerland.



Typeset in 11 pt Times Roman by
C. R. Barber & Partners (Highlands) Ltd, Fort William, Scotland
Printed and bound by
Richard Clay Ltd, Bungay, Suffolk

*To*
*Geraldine Beskin*

# Contents

# Introduction

'Let No Man Enter This Place, Save His Hands Be Pure'

That quotation, inscribed over the entrance to the temple of Apollo guarding the cave of the Delphic Oracle, gave some indication of the attitude displayed by the ancient Greeks towards the priests, priestesses and sibyls whose oracular utterances in the form of advice and prophecy were regarded as direct messages from the divine gods, and their messengers sacrosanct.

In ancient Rome, the establishment of the College of Augurs, whose priests predicted events by the practice of studying the habits of birds, elevated soothsaying to a semi-divine status. Other practices in the ancient world included the study of natural phenomena, the entrails of animals, the pattern of lightning flashes and the interpretation of dreams. Those who were fortunate enough to have acquired an education mastered the age-old science of astrology, and many a wealthy Roman family employed a personal astrologer or consulted a seer regularly. Both of these categories of people would have been regarded as possessors of an unusual but nevertheless recognised and accepted ability, and accorded respect for their skills.

It is only comparatively late in our history, when the early Christian Church was struggling to maintain its hold in Europe by stamping out all traces of the old religion, that Saturn became confused with Satan; and the word witch, deriving from the Wicca, the wise or all-seeing, gained the connotation of godlessness and evil. From there, it was but a short step from nature-worship, to devil-worship and the seers, those gifted with pre-natural insight, became obscured in a cloud of fear and superstition.

So, for many centuries, psychic abilities lay under a cloud. It was something which the frightened possessor regarded as being from the Devil himself, or, in the hardier souls, lay accepted but undisclosed for fear of persecution. In the latter so-called 'Age of Reason', it was often regarded as something which must be kept well hidden for fear of ridicule. It is only in the last forty years that an open interest has been evinced in the occult, and great advances made in the study of the mysterious powers of the mind, although for twice that number of years psychic and spiritualist societies had been conducting experiments with striking but little publicised results. The scientific methods of Dr Rhine at Duke University in America have proved conclusively that there exists a telepathic ability termed extra sensory perception, and also that hand in hand with this sense, there is another which incorporates the ability to look into the future and sometimes to look backwards into the past. These have not, as yet, been fully explained, but the results have been so conclusive, the tests so fool-proof and the methods so scientific, that they cannot be ignored, dismissed or laughed away as many older conclusive experiments were.

Let's call it, for want of a better description, the sixth sense which it may very well be. I believe it to be present in a large percentage of the population in varying degrees, but in most cases awaiting development and guidance to enable it to be used properly. For some psychics, this sense is so overwhelmingly strong, there is no need for such devices as cards, cups or crystal balls which are, basically, a method of trancing the mind or a guideline for the intuition. For it is when the mind's mental activity is quietened, and the point of focus set, that the intuition or sixth sense fed by the supra-conscious comes into play. The symbols of these cards or tea leaves act as guide lines for the messages which come through clairvoyantly.

The most fascinating, bewildering and mysterious of these divinatory aids are the ancient Tarot cards. Their meanings rise high above mundane material existence. They are concerned with the less transitory values, the more important moral triumphs and failures that make up man's progress through life. Their spiritual significance lifts them above the mere fortune-telling device. Their accent is on spiritual growth, evolution, Karmic forces and cosmic consciousness, and must never be approached in a spirit of levity or used for selfish personal gain.

Everything about them is intriguing and mysterious, from their known sources, their purpose, their underlying philosophy, their history, even to the origin of their name. These have all been subjects of many conflicting and confusing theories, written by learned authorities for nearly two hundred years.

I hope, in this book, not to further confuse the reader, for I am not adding anything new to the study of Tarot. Rather I am hoping to give a concise and simplified account of the history, the different authors and readers, the possible origin of the symbology, the collective meanings of the twenty-two picture cards of the Major Arcana and fifty-six suit cards of the Minor Arcana, and basic easy methods of divination for the layman who wants to learn as much as he can about the Tarot cards in the shortest time and in terms he can understand. I am indebted to many authorities for the material collected and have gained experience, over many years as a clairvoyant, in the methods of divination, but humbly consider myself still a student of the Tarot, for the more I learn, the more there is to learn about these fascinating cards. At the back of the book I have placed a list of books on various aspects of the Tarot for those who wish to pursue the subject further.

*Chapter One*

# The History of the Tarot

On the stage of medieval Europe, paganism still postured from behind a variety of masks and disguises. Although the Christian Church had adopted many of its rituals and transformed many of its beliefs, it kept a wary eye on certain practices considered godless and suspect. One of these was gambling, for luck was still equated in many men's minds with the pagan god Lok, and the Church distrusted the pagan appeal that fate or Kismet made to the senses. All forms of gambling were abhorred but particularly that of card playing. It is an interesting pointer that the word sorcery came from the Latin word to cast lots and the Semitic word for sorcery 'naib' derived from the word meaning card play or gambling. This attitude still lingered in the days of the Puritans who, sensing the pagan defiance behind the Tarot imagery, called it 'the Devil's picture book'.

The first recorded diatribe against card play is attributed to a monk at Brefeld, Switzerland, in 1377. This seems by description to refer not to the picture cards of the 22 Major Arcana trumps or 'triumphs' as they were called, but to a pack of fifty six suit cards, the derivation of our modern pack of gambling cards. It is thought that the two packs were amalgamated at a later date, and not until 1450, by the writings of another monk, a Franciscan friar in Northern Italy, was the entire set referred to in yet another exhortation against the evils of gambling and the pagan imagery of the picture cards.

The earliest recorded purchase of cards was found in the ledgers of the Dukedom of Brabant in 1379 and in the same year card play was described at a fete in Brussels, but the fullest description of a purchase of three packs of cards was made by the court treasurer of Charles VI of France in 1392. They had been commissioned by a famous artist thought to be Gringonneur, and were painted on vellum, edged with gold and covered with silver, lapis lazuli and a dark red pigment fancifully called 'mummy's dust.' Seventeen cards thought to be from this set in the Bibliotheque Nationale in Paris are now considered to be of a later manufacture.

Although cards were banned in Regensberg, Germany, as early as 1378, such was their universal appeal that by 1380 they were permitted by the code of Nuremburg and by 1393 were listed as among the permitted games in Florence. However, the hard-headed French passed a ban in Paris in 1397, preventing commoners from gambling with cards on working days. A typically English decree came later in England, in 1463, passed by an equally hard-headed King Edward IV. This was not to ban card playing but to prohibit imports of cards from foreign countries, such a commercial success had they become. By this time, master card-makers had appeared for the first time in the Brabant guild registers and women card-painters were known to be registered at Nuremburg. This industry had become possible by the introduction of wood block printing in Europe in the early fifteenth century and saw the end of the flimsy cheap stencilled packs. The wealthier section of the community had always been in the practice of commissioning artists to design Tarot packs, and indeed many famous artists found time in the midst of their larger commissions to create their own card packs. Dürer came to Italy, saw the Minchiate pack and upon his return to Germany produced his own version. It is a fascinating thought that today we still have some of these medieval designs, for the almost unaltered Marseilles pack was based on early wood-cuts.

Preserved from the wrath of St Bernardin of Sienna, who made a public proclamation against cards in 1423, and doubtless consigned many such exquisite packs to the flames in righteous wrath, the Visconti pack, created by Marziona de Tartona for Filipo Marie Visconti, the Duke of Milan, is perhaps the most famous of all traditional Tarot packs known today. Many other packs were designed for the great dynastic families of northern Italy, and one such, the Bologna, was probably the object of St Bernardin's indignation. It was designed by Francesco Fibbia, the Prince of Pisa, during his exile in Bologna, and is said by some to be the originator of the Tarot pack in its present form. However, it contained no Minor Arcana under six, (a practice that many fortune-tellers even today follow) and was called the *Tarochinno* or little Tarot pack and obviously designed for a game of his own invention. The Visconti pack, it is said, copied his conception but added the missing numeral cards. Certainly the Prince of Pisa was given great honours and it is suggested that he received them for his idea of combining the suit cards with an older pack of picture cards, used perhaps for some purpose other than gambling, or invented the Tarot symbols themselves, using something else as a model. His symbolism was striking, the Major Arcana seemingly denoting man's spiritual progress in material existence, and his sequence culminated at 'the Judgement', giving force to this moralistic theme. Yet again there is another opinion which concerns the four Tarot cards in the Musee Carrer which are thought not to be French as accepted, but Venetian, and these are considered by some to be the parents of all the other packs.

Another Italian pack is the Florentine or Minchiate pack. This consists of the regular seventy eight Tarot cards, plus the twelve astrological signs, the four basic elements, earth, air, fire and water, and the four virtues, faith, hope, charity, and prudence.

These three Italian packs form the basis of the modern Tarot packs available today. There are many different packs, – some national, such as the French Marseilles pack; German and Swiss which carry for the suit devices bells, acorns, roses and shields; some from the Psychic Institute and various spiritual orders; the Etteilla Tarot; and the Pamela Coleman Smith cards designed for Waite, influenced by Rosicrucian doctrine.

However, there is one pack in existence, known as the Baldini pack, but once thought to have been executed by Mantegna, which differs in many ways from the accepted Tarot and was considered to have been used as a memory system in a quasi-theological game during a seven month Ecclesiastical Council in 1459, to relieve the tedium for the Pope and his two Cardinals. This set made free use of pagan symbology, and consisted of fifty cards of five denaries of ten cards each, embracing in picture form the conditions of life, the liberal arts and sciences, the virtues, the heavens and the muses. One authority, Romain Merlin, asserted that this set dated from the fourteenth century and others copied and diverged from it. It has certain similarities with the pack of designed for Charles VI of France, and Merlin's view was that Tarot cards were well known in Europe long before Gringonneur designed this set for the French king. However, as we have learned before, it has now been established that the seventeen cards thought to be from this early French set are considerably later in period and of possible Italian origin.

The Baldini pack is interesting because it is said to represent a mnemonic system, and this type of memory aid is said by Paul Huson,a leading modern authority on the occult, to have been the original purpose of the Major Arcana. This theory seems to me to be more acceptable than many high-flown esoteric explanations given in the past for the conception of the Tarot, but the arguments make fascinating reading so let us trace the confusing and conflicting theories of scholars from the discovery of these cards up to the present day.

*Chapter Two*

# The Theories

In one of the nine works of a massive volume, *Le monde primitif*, French writer Antoine de Gebelin, amateur scholar, antiquarian and historian, wrote in 1781 a section called 'Le Jeu de Tarots', dealing with the Tarot cards. The author had come across these a few years earlier, and had become excited by their symbology which he attributed to the occult beliefs of ancient Egypt. He was interested in everything pertaining to ancient Egypt, as were many scholars of the neo-classical period, and as the Rosetta Stone was not to be discovered for another eighteen years, he was safe to assert that these cards were the remains of the sacred Book of Thoth. He discovered that the cards were relatively unknown in France, except in the southern country districts and Marseilles, but that they were of considerable antiquity and had existed in Belgium, Italy, Germany and Spain, both as a divinatory method and as a game of chance, for hundreds of years. He studied the methods, and the attributed meanings, but reconstructed the cards, altering some of the symbolism and the meanings to fit in with both his Egyptian theory and his philosophy as a high grade Mason.

A contemporary of his and disciple, Alliette, or Etteilla, as he later respelled his name, a Parisian barber, published his own work on the Tarot two years after de Gebelin's, and further accentuated the divinatory aspect of the cards. His knowledge of the occult was mere surface gleanings compared to de Gebelin's, and he lacked the other's spirituality, but he possessed a strong commercial sense and a flair for showmanship. He became one of the foremost fortune-tellers in France. He styled himself 'priest of the occult' and produced two more books which were written, he claimed, by seventeen Magi of the Temple of Fire on the borders of the Levant. His books appealed to the masses but the pack of cards he produced, which is still in use today, is considered by many later authorities to have been a debased version of de Gebelin's. Although he claimed that his innovations were but corrections of the inevitably corrupted Egyptian designs, they are said to be a tasteless amalgamation of contemporary French emblems and traditional symbols. He added nothing new to the solution of the Tarot mystery, merely promoting the Egyptian theory and adding his own rather suspect designs and interpretations of the meanings.

The newly-awakened interest in these cards resulted naturally in a spate of fortune-tellers, although there had been books published on fortune-telling in France as early as 1634, using cards and dice. After Etteilla came two more renowned seers, both authors. They were Julia Orsini and Marie le Normand. The latter achieved renown by her prediction of Napoleon's marriage to Josephine, and the former published a book claimed to be based on papers left with Mademoiselle le Normand by the same Josephine. Her methods were unique, and she is said to have needed only three cards on which to base an entire reading. Claiming among her clients such personages as the Tzar of Russia, she was greatly in demand and accordingly set her fees very high. She published a book on card reading methods and created her own pack based loosely on the Tarot. These can be purchased today, and some of her methods are still used.

Then came a wave of more rational scholars who disagreed with the rather romantic Egyptian theory. One Samuel Singer echoed another earlier Italian writer, Covelluzo, who claimed in his book written in the fifteenth century, that the cards entered Italy from Arabia in the fifteenth century. Two more dissenters were Duchesne and William Chatto, who agreed that the Tarot was European in origin and the Egyptian theory high-flown romance.

Next, an interesting suggestion developed into a contra-theory when P. B'Oiteau D'Ambley wrote a treatise on playing cards and identified the Tarot with the Bohemian gypsies, after detecting what he considered to be a slight oriental influence. This he attributed to the transit of the gypsies through India on their way to Europe. Three years later a more formidable exponent of the Roman theory, J. A. Vaillant, who had lived with the gypsies and was considered to be a leading authority on the Romany language, history and culture, wrote a book suggesting that the Tarot originated with the gypsies. Later scholars seem to be of the opinion that although the Romanies may have spread the divinatory lore of the Tarot throughout Europe from a very early time, there is little evidence to support Vaillant's assertions. Romain Merlin, in 1869, refuted this theory by stating that the Tarot cards were in existence in Europe long before the arrival of the gypsies, which is recorded as 1417 at Luneberg. However, there are indications that wandering tribes of Romanies were familiar in Europe long before that date, and it is an interesting fact that the Romany word for deck of cards is Tar. This is even more striking when we find that the language of these people derives from the purest form of Sanskrit, itself the oldest of the Indo-European languages and the same word in the old language is Taru. The ancient belief that the Romanies came from Egypt (our English word derives from the word Egyptian), is thought-provoking according to one brilliant authority, Paul Huson. He points out that the patron saint of the Romanies, Saint Sara, has her shrine, Les Saintes Maries de la Mer, in the Camargue, and this rests upon what legend has it is the site of an ancient altar of the Roman god Mithras. Mithras assimilated the Egyptian god of the dead into his pantheon, and that god's name was Sarapis.

According to another modern writer, Wenzell Brown, the gypsies have always claimed that they possess a secret book more ancient than any known, which is the only true guide to fortune-telling by the cards. No copy of this has ever come to light, and it seems that the divinatory methods of the gypsies are handed down in an oral tradition. The same author states that in his belief some version of the Tarot cards were the tablets (referred to in the Book of Moses) which the Israelites consulted.

But again, a hundred years ago, all roads seemed to lead back to ancient Egypt, and the next scholar who published his works in the middle of the last century sustained this theory, embellished by additions of his own. He could be said to have shaped the modern attitude to the Tarot – or at least that which prevailed up to the last thirty years. He was Alphonse Constant, better known as Eliphas Levi. First educated in a Catholic order and destined for the Church, he later switched to a study of the occult and published works on magic – aspects of which linked with the Tarot trumps the Major Arcana. His contribution to the subject was to link the meanings of the Tarot trumps with the Hebrew mystical system, first known in Spain in the twelfth century as the Qabbala. He also linked each Tarot trump with the letters of the Hebrew alphabet, each of which has a mystical meaning, and the emblems of the four suits, as well as the four elements fire, water, earth and air, and the four Hebraic symbols of the divine name, Yod, Heh, Vau and Yahveh. He considered the cards a key to ancient magic, and influenced by Vaillant, later considered them to have been introduced into Europe by the gypsies. In turn, another later occultist, Oswald Wirth, designed a pack of cards based on Levi's ideas, but Levi's greatest exponent was Papus who published the *Tarot of the Bohemians* in the 1890s. This work incorporated Wirth's cards with Levi's theories and added a new dimension of meaning to the Minor Arcana, based on the Hebrew system of numbers. He introduced as a basis for the meanings of these cards a system of threes; commencement, apogee and decline. He also edited Ettcilla's earlier work on Tarot – thus saving it from oblivion. Papus, a doctor of medicine, a Rosicrucian, and founder of a school of the occult in Paris, believed that the Major Arcana embodied the spiritual history of man; or the soul of man, coming out from the eternal, passing through material darkness, and emerging into the light again.

Another school of thought evolving in England about this time was due to the foundation of a Rosicrucian type order, 'The Order of the Golden Dawn'. This body correlated the Tarot cards with the Qabbalistic concept of the 'Tree of Life'. This is a mystical diagram of ten stages or aspects in ascending triangles linked together by twenty-two paths, thought of as the 'Anatomy of the Deity' and embracing such concepts as grace, mercy, serenity, victory, splendour and many more. The man largely responsible for this new development was Samuel Mathers, later known as McGregor Mathers, who published a book in which he propounded that the Tarot trumps were in their numerical sequence, a moral treatise on human will and enlightenment. He also incorporated the zodiac and the planets into his credo. This school of thought differed in the order of the cards, and some modern packs today diverge on this point. However, since the early cards differed again in numerical sequence, this is of little significance to the diviner. Whereas some authorities place the Fool at the end of the sequence, or do not number this card, this Order equates it with the Hebrew letter Aleph, the beginning, but number it 'O' – symbol of the eternal. Their pack, created for the members and not for general use, was based on the 'Tree of Life' and its gradations and meanings, allied with the Qabbala. A pack following these lines was published in 1916 by a member of this Order, A. E. Waite, a renowned scholar of the occult. With the help of artist Pamela Coleman Smith, herself a member of the Order of the Golden Dawn, he changed much of the traditional design of the Minor Arcana, by making them picture cards. Later scholars have criticised this departure from tradition, and also his incorporation of Rosicrucian concepts into the meanings of the cards. He re-edited the *Tarot of the Bohemians*, the older work by Papus, but had scant sympathy with the 'Book of Thoth' concept, and considered that although Papus was on the right track when he asserted that the Tarot was a collection of esoteric writings, he did not delve deeply enough. In his opinion, the Tarot symbology was universal, their truths to be found on two levels, and the divinatory aspects incidental and unimportant. His was the suggestion that the two packs were originally combined by the Prince of Pisa. Another view of his was that the symbols of the Minor Arcana are linked with the Holy Grail. Other scholars have noticed the similarity of these emblems with the Irish magical treasure, the spear of Lug, the cauldron of Dagda, the sword of Nuada and the stone of Fal, but Waite leans more to the Arthurian legends and says the spear of Lug could also be the spear of Longinus in the legend of the Holy Grail. Strangely, Eden Gray, who has written a manual for fortune-telling based on the Waite-Coleman Smith cards, completely reverses the order of the suits and their accepted tradition of denoting the colouring which indicates our choice of the significator card for the client. However, this is a small point, and the fact that Waite's meanings may differ slightly from the traditional Marseilles pack's interpretation does not really matter. His cards are very beautiful indeed, and helpful for the beginner as the imagery on the suit cards illustrate the basic meaning.

There were other books by members of this Order. One outstandingly different work was produced by Aleister Crowley after he had broken away from the Order of the Golden Dawn and founded his own Order of the Silver Star. This he called ambitiously *The Book of Thoth* and the only new contribution or improvement he made to those works produced by the members of his former Order was to change the order of progression of trumps to make a more convincing correlation with the 'Tree of Life' doctrine. A noted occultist of the 30s P. Ouspensky, did not believe that the cards had any sequential relationship, but rather that each card must be contrasted with another. The Fool is contrasted with card number one, card number two with card number twenty one, card number three with card twenty two and so on. A more modern writer, Sidney Bennett, links the court and other cards with astrology and the seasons. Numerology is also incorporated in this system of reading, by bringing the date of the day and the year to one unit, then linking it with all cards in the Major or Minor Arcana that carry that number. This author asserts that a similar cycle of events will occur on each number one day, (that is – a day of which the date plus the numerals of the year will reduce to the unit one, for instance the twelfth of May 1973) (1 plus 2 plus 5 plus 1 plus 9 plus 7 plus 3 equals 28 equals 2 plus 8 equals 10 equals 1 plus 0 equals 1) and to obtain a forecast you simply check each morning all Major or Minor cards which carry that number, and read the divinatory meaning. Another modern author who relates the Tarot to the seasons and the zodiac is Carlyle A. Pushong, who also has some interesting correlations to make between the Tarot doctrine and Sankara's doctrine of Maya.

He also underlines the philosophy of reincarnation and Karma. Richard Gardner, a noted modern writer and occult scholar, believes that the Minor Arcana symbolises the four elementals composing all manifestations, (fire, water, earth and air) in different quantities according to their numerical value; and the Major Arcana gives us a pattern for living by showing us our hidden potential and the restrictions which prevent our succeeding. He believes that two dynamics motivate us and all around us; fire and water. Fire is equated always with the masculine religions and water with the feminine. These two elements react upon earth and air, and the four elements which we all have present within each of us must be balanced harmoniously in order for us to live happily and achieve our full potential. The suit of Cups he maintains is ruled by water; the Wands by fire; the Sword by air; and the Pentacle by earth.

The modern view, that the Tarot was a memory system used by one of the Gnostic sects, has been presented skilfully and convincingly by Paul Huson and discussed intelligently and sympathetically by Alfred Douglas, both brilliant modern authorities on the Tarot. This latter-day theory is the most fascinating of all in my opinion, and in many ways the most convincing. Possibly Harold Bayley first came to this conclusion when, examining a parchment of Albigensian origin, he noted that the Eucharistic symbol depicted thereon showed a remarkable resemblance to the symbol for the Ace of Cups of the Tarot. He concluded that the Tarot has evolved as a secret language of the Albigensian sect. But why secret, and what is Albigensian?

Again we have to return to medieval Europe and from there to the excitement of the Renaissance. A great revival of learning led to the classical past being rediscovered. Boundaries were widening in every way. New seaways were being discovered and travellers like Marco Polo had set the world record for distance and opened up a new world. Byzantium's influence was waning while the cities of northern Europe were dominating the trade routes. The Italian and Venetian ports were becoming great centres of commerce, busy bustling cities responsible for transporting armies, victualling the crusaders and accommodating within their walls many different nationalities. The Italian merchants now travelled as far as England, Russia and Spain, while the sea captains and traders learned first-hand of the strange customs and alien philosophies of China and India, and with the cargoes and the profits came new and disturbing ideas. This knowledge began to spread, and the multi-racial nature of the cities bred an interest in foreign lands and begat a tolerance that drew scholars from every land to study at the centres of the new learning. A growing interest in the literature of other lands caused centres of translation to spring up in France and Spain, and scholars then for the first time had access to the philosophy and legends of many cultures. All kinds of subjects were translated, ranging from treatises on Arabian astrology to Christian writings, neo-Christian subjects, classical literature. Even a French version of the Arthurian legend found its way over the channel. Pagan gods and goddesses, the heroes of legend and song, were permeating the literature of the period. This preoccupation with the classical, its philosophies and religious beliefs, seems to have sprung from a universal sense of failure. The established religions had not satisfied an inner hunger for spiritual development, and a consequent thirst for knowledge arose and with it came the search for more lasting values. The Gnostic sects had flourished in Alexandria as early as the second century A.D. They were break-offs from the orthodox Christian religions and were considered by the established church to be heretical servants of the Devil. The word Gnostic comes from the Greek word for knowledge, and this name was applied loosely to a number of separate sects, all of whom had descended from the Paulisians, an Armenian Christian heretical sect whose beliefs were a mixture of Persian, Chaldean, Indian, Egyptian, Hebrew and Christian beliefs, laced heavily with Greek philosophy. There were sects whose only real difference was regional and they were named after their location: for example as the Bogomils, and their offshoots the Waldenses and the Albigenses, or as these were also designated, the Cathars. This last sect, whose name meant 'pure', were dualists who believed in two opposing forces for good and evil, Christ and the Demi-Urge. They rejected resurrection both of Christ and of themselves, and believed that the Demi-Urge created the body, in which is contained a Divine Spark, the godhead, or the opposing good, which can only be set free through knowledge and consequent enlightenment. The medieval Church, though not averse to borrowing some of the customs and emblems of these sects, endeavoured to stamp out all practices considered to be anti-Christian, and drove the Gnostics underground or exterminated them altogether.

With this suspicious attitude and rigid persecution of anything outside the teaching of the Church, the centres of learning narrowed down to the cloisters. Literacy was rare even among the wealthier classes, and most of the teaching lay in the hands of the clergy. Much of this pagan literature was consigned to the flames, but a considerable amount of the dangerous heretical works on magic was retained and studied by scholarly clerics with an occult bent. These gave the explanation or excuse that the Church must fully understand the older doctrines in order to know thoroughly the enemy it was fighting.

Such ancient magical works as *The Greater Key*, *The Book of Solomon*, *The Picatrix* and the *Grimoires*, which described spells, gave instructions for the conjuring up of spirits, the controlling of demons and the fashioning of powerful magical talismans and found their way into the monasteries as well as books on alchemy and astrology. Because writing was a much prized but rare skill in these days there evolved a system of memory training in the form of a series of pictorial images arranged in a certain order. These were a kind of mental shorthand, each image itself a stimulus to release given information previously memorised. One section of opinion had long considered memory-aids a direct path to the Devil. St Thomas Aquinas condemned the *Ars Notoria*, a Mnemonic system for both its pagan imagery and its underlying reliance of the powers of magic. The alchemist had considered memory training a stimulus to the unconscious, and the use of these techniques plus the intoning of certain magical formulae was considered a method of invoking the supernatural. One fragment of a memory system used in the monasteries still in existence today is the Stations of the Cross.

Paul Huson believes that the Tarot trumps may well have been some such memory system, deriving from a classical mystery cult, based on Isis and Hermes Trismegistos (known in Egypt as Thoth), the god that the Gnostics claimed was the originator of the twin sciences of alchemy and astrology.

There has been a view put forward that the Tarot cards were the invention of the Knights Templar. This was an ascetic military order founded by Hugh de Payens in 1188, with eight fellow knights, to protect pilgrims and guard routes to the Holy Land. However, over the centuries the Order had become extremely powerful and too wealthy. Philip XIV of France in 1307 brought charges of heresy against the Order, had many members tortured into making false confessions, confiscated their property and had their leader publicly burned at the stake. All the other centres in other countries were treated in a similar manner and the Order disbanded in 1314. It has been suggested that the Templars were worshipping a version of Mithras, the Roman ruler of the sun and war, and the natural divinity for a military order. One link with the Tarot cards is the eighteenth century portrayal of card number fifteen, the Devil, whose imagery is consistent with the Baphomet (the common word for any idol) supposedly worshipped by the Templars. Statues somewhat similar had been found in some of their meeting places, and considered by the Christian Church to represent the Devil, although they were derived from Janus and Saturn.

Another interesting theory on the creation of the Major Arcana takes us back to medieval Italy where a golden strand in the fabric of life in the Italian cities was the pageants and festival processions. These were called Triumphs and were often commissioned by one of the ruling princes, and could be in honour of a visiting dignitary or a Saint's day, or sometimes to celebrate a dynastic marriage, or again, to please the Church. Originally of a religious nature, possibly stemming from ancient mystery plays, they were usually dramatic tales with a moral theme. They developed into such costly and elaborate tableaux that artists were commissioned to design them and engineers to create the mechanism of animation. Leonardo da Vinci designed one such Triumph, and from the fourteenth century there existed a game using the twenty-two picture cards, called Triumphs. It is a possibility that the Tarot cards themselves may have been the commemoration in miniature of one such memorable procession, perhaps given by the artist to his wealthy patron, or commissioned by the patron himself, or perhaps they themselves were used as an integral part of the pageant or Triumph in long-ago Italy.

*Chapter Three*

# The Major Arcana

## ITS SYMBOLOGY AND MEANINGS

The Tarot Pack consists of seventy eight cards in all. The twenty-two picture cards are called the Major Arcana, or the trumphs of 'triumphs'. The fifty-six suit cards are divided into four suits and are called the Minor Arcana. The Major Arcana are numbered to twenty-one. The Fool or Jester is usually unnumbered, although some packs number this card 'O', and some Tarot packs place it at the end, rather than at the beginning of the sequence. But this does not matter for the purpose of divination.

## CARD NUMBER ONE

## THE MAGICIAN, MAGUS OR PAGAD

*Origin*

This card is sometimes known as the Magus, after the leader of the Mithraic community whose task it was to introduce candidates into the mysteries and into the presence of the Gods. He is linked with Mercury, guide to the souls in the underworld, and messenger of the gods. Mercury was gifted with divination, but was known as something of a super salesman, a sharp operator with 'the gift of the gab'. The word mercator, to sell, comes from him, and words were peculiarly his own property, for he was renowned for his propensity for disseminating news and gossip. He loved anything new, particularly ideas, and ruling as he did all kinds of mental dexterity, it is not surprising that quick thinking, guile, cunning and trickery become associated with Hermes or Mercury. The eternal mischief maker, his later prototypes were Harlequin, Puck, the Elfin Cobbler, the Little Red Sprite of Florence and Robin Goodfellow of England. Often he is depicted in Italian packs as a cobbler and is known as *Il Bagattel* or *Bagatto*; this word derives from *Bagatt*, meaning gossip, and is the derivation of another name for his card, THE PAGAD.

*Description*

This card shows a young man dressed as either a cobbler or a magician. If depicted as a cobbler, he wears multicolored garments and a large brimmed hat, shaped a little like a figure eight lying on its side. He holds a small rod or tool in his left hand, and stands behind a table on which lie various tools of the cobbler's trade. The figure eight shape is said by some scholars to represent the Cosmic Lemniscate, a figure considered by ancient Egyptians to be the symbol of eternal life, and the rod is possibly derived from the Caduceus, the traditional staff of

Mercury. As a magician, he wears a white robe, blue sash and red cloak. He holds a wand high in his right hand, and points his left hand to the earth. Above his head is the figure eight shape, the *lemniscate*, which other scholars consider derived from head-wear similar to that of Mercury, which was often portrayed on the earliest Tarot cards. At his feet are lilies and roses.

*Symbolic Meaning*

This first card has a dual meaning which some packs of cards point up by depicting the magician's girdle as a serpent holding its tail in its mouth. This is the occult symbol for knowledge and duality. On the highest level, it symbolizes the seeker of spiritual truth, the union of the personal and the divine, power, subtlety and diplomacy; but on the other level it symbolizes the use and abuse of occult power for selfish ends, domination, deceit, trickery, devious methods and lies.

*Actual Meaning*

The Commencement card: initiative, will, self awareness, the ability to translate thought into action, willingness to take risks resulting in triumph, the guidance of occult forces, learning, new skills, new facts, new careers.

*Reversed Meaning*

Delay, uncertainty, guile, trickery, misuse of occult powers.

*Combinations*

When this card is placed near THE DEVIL or THE WHEEL, it has the effect of delaying events or causing hesitation. If placed next to DEATH, it cancels itself out.

## CARD NUMBER TWO

## THE HIGH PRIESTESS OR PAPESSA

*Origin*

Juno, sister of the earth mother and also her alter ego, Hera the mistress. The pomegranate often displayed in early cards shows the link with Persephone, queen of the dead, known as Juno Inferna, Juno's dark aspect. When taken to Italy she became Iana, and Juno, Diana and Iana all come from the root *div* meaning to shine. She symbolized the moon. When the Egyptian culture was absorbed by the Romans, she was equated with Isis and carried the assurance of life after death. In many fourteenth century manuscripts, Luna was depicted as an abbess which was also a popular idea in Celtic mythology, where both Brigid, the Celtic queen of heaven and Morrigan (Morgan le Fay's derivation) who was the counterpart of Persephone were portrayed in ecclesiastical garb. The Pope Joan legend, adapted from an earlier legend by a thirteenth century Dominican monk, derives from a legend of Juno. Juno was often used to invoke memory in ancient talismans which gave oracular and prophetic power to the wearer The HIGH PRIESTESS title came from the revival of classical interest in the eighteenth century and refers to the role of the priestess who acted the part of the goddess during the Greek mysteries.

*Description*

A seated female figure, crowned or wearing a crescent moon head dress, holds a partly unrolled scroll which is half hidden by her garments. She wears a solar or ansated cross at her breast. In some packs she sits in between two pillars, one black, one white, which some occultists claim represent the Pillars of Boaz and Jakin, the negative and positive elements. The palm leaves and pomegranates often depicted in this card are said to represent the masculine and the feminine elements of creativity. Other cards picture her with a crescent moon at her feet and wearing a horned head dress, symbolizing Isis, the goddess of the moon. The book is thought to be the Tora or divine law by some authorities, and these cards often have the letters T.O.R.A. depicted on the scroll.

*Symbolic Meaning*

As contrasted with THE MAGICIAN, she is passive, the female element representing spiritual enlightenment and the inner life. She stands for esoteric truths, hidden knowledge, mystery, silence, the unrevealed future, hidden influences, philosophy and learning.

*Actual Meaning*

This card stands for occult studies, creative talent, divination, mysticism, esteoric knowledge and a thirst for learning. It brings satisfaction from studies, can often denote the teacher, means hidden things revealed, safety and spiritual protection, duality, mystery and cultural advancement.

*Reversed Meaning*

Sensuous pleasure, mere surface learning, other things delayed but not weakened.

*Combinations*

If placed next to THE WHEEL and both cards are upright it adds strength and balance to the latter and means a certain recompense in a law suit or petition which could seem hopeless at the outset. When reversed, in the same position, this means a blighted future, loss of stability and a violent upheaval. If reversed and followed by an upright TEMPERANCE, it means that future prospects are very dark, for this combination brings almost unconquerable obstacles, bewilderment and the inability to act or find a solution.

## CARD NUMBER THREE

### THE EMPRESS

*Origin*

The Earth Mother, Demeter, Eleusis, Vesta or Bona Dea. The mother of Dionysus, himself the central figure in the Greek mysteries. She shares with other traditions, the death of her son brought about by his enemies, the loss, unobtainable quest for life and happiness, and the joy after mourning, when her son is reborn as a new entity. She represents fruitfulness, gestation, nourishment and is nature abundant.

*Description*

Seated on a throne she holds a sceptre in her left hand, in some cards ornamented with a crux ansata, others a cross surmounted by a ball. On her right there sits a shield, decorated with an eagle or a cross. She wears a crown or a diadem on her long abundant hair, and in some cards, she is depicted wearing a necklace of pearls and flowing robes that hint at coming motherhood. Often she is seen with trees behind her, corn waving around her, and water at her feet.

*Symbolic Meaning*

The productive vivifying life principle, the seed-to-flower process, fertility and fecundity. As opposed to the logical intellect she symbolizes spiritual feeling and intuitive emotion. She also stands for progeny and growth, harmony in nature. To the artist, she brings inspiration and energy necessary for creative endeavour, and to the farmer she brings growth and abundance. To the lover she brings marriage, often a wealthy union, and children.

*Actual Meaning*

A strong force, a natural course of events which proves

beneficial, domestic stability and harmony, the good life. She brings material wealth and marriage, often wealthy; a kind benefactor, she brings good health after illness. She also symbolizes mother love, children, artistic creation, land tillage and abundance.

*Reversed Meaning*
Luxury loving laziness, maternal tyranny, domestic upheaval, war or destruction, wasting of talents or resources. An inevitable event will be slightly delayed.

*Combinations*
When this card precedes THE MAGICIAN, diplomacy brings the means of success. If this card precedes THE CHARIOT there will be a decisive victory in the material sense. If this card is reversed in the same position, the victory will be delayed but inevitable.

## CARD NUMBER FOUR

## THE EMPEROR

*Origin*
This image traces back to the horned gods, and is associated with Priapus. It is possibly directly conceived from an ancient talisman found in the Arab *Grimoire* and *The Picatrix*, the sacred book of esoteric magic, which shows a crowned king, sitting on a throne, a globe beneath his feet and a raven on his bent forearm. It was believed that this talisman brought the wearer great power, potency and honours. Some medieval artists are thought to have incorporated Charlemagne himself into this design, as Byzantian influence shown in the dress of this card and its female counterpart THE EMPRESS, appear in some of the earlier Tarot packs.

*Description*

A crowned masculine kingly figure is seated on a throne which is decorated sometimes with rams' heads, the symbol of Mars, or a lion's head (the symbol of Leo and the sun). He holds a sceptre in his right hand, sometimes decorated with a crux ansata, the symbol of eternal life, and a shield sits at his right side, featuring either an eagle or a cross. Sometimes he is depicted with a beard, a symbol of wisdom and endurance. Some packs show him with feet planted firmly on land while mountains rise in the distance, representing terrestrial domination and unyielding power.

*Symbolic Meaning*

As contrasted with THE EMPRESS, whose domination is of hearth and home, and the forces of nature, THE EMPEROR is the dominating male force. He stands for rule of the masses, governorship, temporal power, logic, analysis, intellectual ability and will-power.

*Actual Meaning*

Wealth and power of the temporal kind, leadership, stability, creative energy, mental activity, knowledge through experience, intelligence dominating passion.

*Reversed Meaning*

The passions triumph over the intelligence, justice, possibly pity and mercy shown, clemency, loss of wealth, emotional immaturity, weakening of power.

*Combinations*

When in front of THE WORLD, and if upright, this means a *lull in war*, a state of truce, or a transient peace. If reversed, the card used to mean *war on a national scale*, conflict for the individual and loss of power of position *on a world scale*.

## CARD NUMBER FIVE

## THE POPE OR HIEROPHANT

*Origin*

Jupiter, the all-forgiving father to whom the guilty turned for forgiveness, through the intercession of the priests. A similar talisman in *The Picatrix* in Babylonian times showed the crowded figure seated on what the quabalists called the Merkebah Throne, sometimes depicted as a chariot, surrounded by the four Holy Living Creatures referred to in Ezekiel. It was thought to give the wearer or the possessor the key to hidden knowledge, spiritual healing and regeneration, also inspiration and genius.

*Description*

Medieval artists often depicted him as the Pope or a monk, but the fourteenth century Visconti pack shows the god Jupiter, while the Florentine Minchiate pack depicts the Pope carrying a globe surmounted by an eagle. He sits between two pillars wearing a pontiff's crown and carries a sceptre or a triple cross in his left hand, while his right hand is lifted in the sign of benediction. He sometimes wears a Maltese cross or wears gloves and slippers embroidered with them. Some packs feature the crossed keys, the symbols of hidden doctrine and authority. In front of him kneel penitents, or priests. The two pillars, a recurring theme of the Tarot, are said by some scholars to represent the pull in opposite directions, the freedom of choice of the individual of the straight and narrow or the broad path.

*Symbolic Meaning*

In contrast with the preceding card of temporal rule, and with the PAPESSA OR HIGH PRIESTESS who denotes hidden esoteric knowledge, this card stands for spiritual domination and traditional teachings for the masses. He rules over the externals of religion and his teaching is both practical and oral.

*Actual Meaning*

Preference for ritual, the established forms of religion and teachings, conventional adherence to established forms, desire for social approval, secrets revealed, scientific or religious vocation. This is the inspirational card of genius, particularly for those connected with the performing arts.

*Reversed Meaning*

Gullibility, delayed ambitions, unconventionality, a late vocation, adoption of modern ideas and innovations, craft, guile and distortion of truth, and treachery.

*Combinations*

When THE EMPEROR and THE HIEROPHANT come together it means a struggle within the enquirer's soul between materialistic and spiritual desires. The outcome will depend upon which card comes first. If both cards are reversed, and THE HIEROPHANT preceding THE EMPEROR, wealth will be lost through pride and failure through lack of knowledge will be possible. If the other way round, this wealth and power will be lost through the abandonment of skills or through lack of learning.

## CARD NUMBER SIX

## THE LOVERS

*Origin*

The origin of this card explains the rather bewildering additional meanings of trial and choice attributed to it. It originally depicted the Judgement of Paris, when Eros, the mischievous son of the goddess Aphrodite, so blinded the eyes of Paris with love that in choosing the fairest of Hera, Athena and Aphrodite, he gave the golden apple to the latter and incurred the wrath and enmity of the other two goddess. The earlier card portrayed all three goddeses, but the later ones only two, with Eros hovering above with his quiver full of arrows tipped with gold and lead. The gold-tipped arrows were the shafts of love, and the leaden-tipped the stings of disillusion. A popular Venus or love talisman in *The Picatrix* showed a naked maiden wreathed in myrtle and roses, holding a mirror, and tethered by a golden chain to a handsome young man who stood beside her stroking her long flowing hair. Above them, of course, floated a plump little boy with his bow and arrow. This talisman, fashioned when Venus was ascending the first ten degrees of Taurus, Pisces or Leo, was said to bring beauty, happiness and love.

*Description*

There have been many changes in the form of this card since De Gebelin depicted it as married life, and Papus followed it with a picture of domestic felicity in the form of a family of mother, father and son, but in the earlier Florentine decks, Paris himself is shown kneeling at the feet of the goddesses, sometimes holding the golden apple, sometimes without it. The more modern decks portray either two women, disparate often in either age or dress, or a youth standing between two women who seem to portray vice and virtue, or simply two lovers hand in hand, with mischievous Cupid hovering overhead in the act of releasing the arrow. He is usually nestling on a fleecy cloud or portrayed in a sunburst, looking rather amused at the predicament of the young man who seems to have a difficult choice. Waite's LOVERS trump shows the Rosicrucian influence, for he has an angel apparently uniting a couple; the man, standing in front of the Tree of Life, has only eyes for the woman, but the woman, standing in front of the Tree of Knowledge, looks at the angel for guidance.

*Symbolic Meaning*

The weighing up of future actions in the light of vice and virtue or positive and negative. The duality of the individual, the freedom of choice; the twin forces of good and evil; the two kinds of love, sacred and profane. The harmony of inner and outer existence.

*Actual Meaning*
Emotional trial resulting in success, choice, love and marriage after choice; trial, moral choice depending upon integrity of client, choice between sacred and profane love; harmony, beauty, attraction, idealistic friendship, vaccillation, instability, hesitation; flash of insight which suddenly solves a problem.

*Reversed Meaning*
Quarrels and partings, the breaking of engagement or marriage, a moral lapse, the wrong choice, wanting the best of both worlds, outside interference, possibly parental, quarrels of offspring.

*Combinations*
THE LOVERS, coming in front of THE CHARIOT, brings revelation of betrayal. If THE CHARIOT comes first, then this means that a sudden departure will put paid to a venture or a romance. If THE LOVERS precedes THE MAGICIAN there will be indecision in commencing a new artistic venture, while if THE LOVERS is reversed in front of THE MAGICIAN this will mean a separation due to indecision and hesitation.

## CARD NUMBER SEVEN

## THE CHARIOT

*Origin*
Zeus, Aries or Mars, son of Jupiter and All-Father. Contrasted with THE POPE who means divine stability, this card represents

the symbol of divine destruction, as also did Thor in Scandinavian mythology, Balor in Irish mythology and Sekhmet in Egyptian. A talisman, very similar to this symbol, fashioned when Mars ascended the first ten degrees of Scorpio, was said by *The Picatrix* to give a man courage and honour in war and success in competitive activities. It featured a canopied chariot drawn by lions. Mediaeval artists often portrayed Mars standing in a chariot, sometimes brandishing a sword or a whip, and sometimes with a halberd. Winged horses often drew the chariot.

*Description*

The fifteenth century cards often depicted Mars brandishing a sword, while the cards attributed to Gringonneur in 1392 show Mars wielding a mighty battleaxe. De Gebelin considered this card Osiris triumphant, or the conquering sun.

The charioteer wears a crown and carries a sceptre denoting victory and triumph. On his shoulders, like epaulettes, lie two faces, thought to represent rule over two opposing forces, while the animals depicted drawing the chariot are sometimes lions, sometimes horses, sometimes a black and white sphinx. These are said to represent the carnal and spiritual forces over which the charioteer has firm control. The four pillars in each corner, upholding the canopy of the chariot, are said to represent the four cardinal elements fire, air, earth, and water. On some cards water, mountains and castles can be seen in the background, and laurel leaves or wreaths and winged suns are often decorating the front of the chariot.

*Symbolic Meaning*

Man conquering on the lower plane, controlling his own nature and mastering the animal passions. The combination of material and physical powers, the union of positive and negative. The triumph of balanced forces, with justice tempered with mercy.

*Actual Meaning*

The card of greatness, not inherited success but success through personal effort. Success for those engaged in artistic pursuits. Triumph over all kinds of difficulties, and health. Achievements, wealth and honour. Speedy travel in luxurious conditions. Unexpected news by word of mouth; the routing of enemies.

*Reversed Meaning*

Warning to conquer the animal passions. Victory through evil methods, unfortunate news or the collapse of plans, the defeat of ambition, ruthlessness, egocentricity.

*Combinations*

If this card is followed by THE MOON, it means that news will come to light that has been kept secret for a long time. If THE CHARIOT follows THE MOON, there will be illness, and if THE MOON is reversed the danger, illness or scandal will not be so strong.

## CARD NUMBER EIGHT

## JUSTICE OR THE BALANCE

*Origin*

Perhaps symbolizing one of the four cardinal virtues or moral precepts of the ancient Greek Stoic philosophers, the first of which, JUSTICE was always depicted as a female. This figure could derive from Themis, who married Zeus and bore Astraea, now our modern constellation Virgo, or could perhaps derive from Athena, goddess of war, whom the Romans called Minerva. She stood, as well as for the more subtle tactics of warfare, for all things pertaining to the mind, for wisdom, vigilance and dispassionate justice. Some of the older cards seem closer to this concept for they depict Justice brandishing a sword, just as Athena brandished her thunderbolt.

*Description*

In some packs, Justice is seen as an angel or a winged figure; in others she is shown sitting on a throne between the customary two pillars between which is stretched a curtain or veil. In one set of cards, she wears a turreted crown, in others a double crown but in all she carries a double-edged sword upraised, in her right hand, at her left, a set of scales or balances. In some packs, there is grass at her feet. She is not blindfolded, as she represents Justice in the all-seeing spiritual sense. In ancient Egyptian belief it was thought that the god Thoth supervised the weighing of the souls of the dead in the Great Balance, on which it was recorded if the heart balanced the symbol of righteousness which was a feather. If it did so, then the soul won its immortality and joined the gods in everlasting life.

*Symbolic Meaning*

Successful combinations, balanced judgement. Modern methods in education replacing outworn creeds. Control. Justice is served.

*Actual Meaning*

Equity, balance, balanced arbitration, the voice of inner conscience, trial and rehabilitation, honesty, justice, good outcome of legal and educational concerns. Good combination of materials, a well balanced outlook, vindication of truth and integrity depending upon the moral position of client.

*Reversed Meaning*

Bigotry, injustice, unjust condemnation, legal tangles, severity, overharsh judgement used against a fellow man.

*Combinations*

When preceding THE HIGH PRIESTESS, this card means secrets

come to light connected with the law. If following, it has much the same meaning, but the facts will have only come to light through legal matters. If both are inverted then events connected with the law or justice will miscarry.

## CARD NUMBER NINE

## THE HERMIT

*Origin*

Saturn, or as he was known in Greece, Kronos, is the origin of this card. The two names became confused with the Roman god Chronus, the god of time. The idea of time became associated with Saturn because longevity, age, slow cautious progress are all connected with this god. Saturn, after years of parental oppression, castrated his own father with an iron sickle, and later devoured his offspring, but was eventually tricked and overpowered by his own son Zeus. The sickle is the derivation of the scythe or reaping hook associated with Old Father Time and with death, and the hour glass with Chronus. Because the element of dark oppression was connected with Saturn early astrologers had little that was cheerful to say about this planet, but instead of gloom and restriction, modern astrologers consider him to be a benevolent taskmaster, who hides a warm heart beneath a cold exterior. Other associations with Saturn seem to be love of learning and cunning, the completion of a cycle of life, wisdom or a great lesson to be learned. Talismans for longevity and wisdom show an old man with an hour glass in hand, often accompanied by a stag, which was another symbol for long life.

*Description*

The early Mantegna decks gave him the title Cronico, and some pictured him as a hermit with an indistinguishable animal at his side. On others he was portrayed as Old Father Time with all the instruments of chronology beside him, while others showed him as a beggar or friar carrying and learning on a staff. The hour glass has now been replaced by a lantern, giving rise to the name 'The Light of the World' bestowed upon his card by early moralists. Levi insisted that this card meant prudence, the hermit travelling the *via prudentia* throughout life, but this was his substitution purely made to fit his sequence of moral progression for system which did not include a PRUDENCE among the trumps. A bearded old man, in cloak and sandals,. carries a lantern before him as if feeling his way by its light. He leans heavily on his staff as he goes on his journeyings. Sometimes he is standing on grassy fields, sometimes mountains tower behind him.

*Symbolic Meaning*

He is an explorer or a venturer. A solitary, making his way carefully, with the help of his staff and by the light of his lantern. He is often bearded, his clock the protection of wisdom, his staff his protection, and the light thought by some authorities to symbolize the light of occult science, his guide. He keeps straight on, letting no one deflect him, albeit slowly and deliberately, taking care that nothing will put out his light, strengthened by the gifts of the divine spirit in his search for wisdom and truth.

*Actual Meaning*

This card takes a lot of its meanings from the surrounding cards. It means no progress without thought or planning. It denotes wisdom from above; silent counsel; the voice of the inner self; a secret revealed; a slowing down of things; deliberation and prudence needed. A beneficial meeting with a wise person. A prospective journey. Attainment after delay.

*Reversed Meaning*

Irksome delays or failure through fear of the unknown, excess fear and caution. Deceit. Stubbornness impeding progress.

*Combinations*
If this card is followed by THE HIGH PRIESTESS, this seems a secret will never be revealed. If THE HIGH PRIESTESS follows THE HERMIT then the secret after patient endeavour will be discovered. If both are inverted this means delay, but revelations nevertheless. If THE HERMIT comes together with THE DEVIL, these two cards influence all the other cards around them. If THE DEVIL precedes THE HERMIT then his power will prevail, but if the other way around, THE HERMIT will shine light on underhand methods and powerful enemies so that good will prevail. If THE DEVIL is inverted, the process will be delayed but eventually right will triumph.

## CARD NUMBER TEN

## THE WHEEL OF FORTUNE

*Origin*
The words fate and prudence have relevance to the origin and derived meanings of this card. Fate, the word from which we obtained fairy, is linked with the Moirae, the triple goddesses of ancient Greece, those three spinners who held the threads of men's destinies in their hands. They gave rise to countless legends of the fairy spinners, and in Saxon times were known as the three Wyrds and as such were the inspiration for Shakespeare's weird sisters. An ancient talisman for the strengthening of the memory and the bestowal of prudence was the symbol of Janus, the Roman god of doorways who had one head looking into the future and the other looking back at the past. Another such image used was of Cerberus, the infernal hound, who had three heads, ruling past, present and future. This seems to have been for THE WHEEL OF FORTUNE portrayed

on the Marseilles pack, for they show either the head of a wolf or an old man on the left of the wheel, denoting memory or the past, a lion or mature man in the centre, denoting intelligence or the present, and the head of a dog or a youth on the right of the wheel, standing for foresight or the future. Some later talismans giving prudence, showed a female figure holding a spiked wheel. The wheel on this trump possibly derives from Ixion, who after being caught in dalliance with the wife of Zeus, was bound to a fiery wheel to spin throughout all eternity. A popular concept of Satan in mediaeval times was a wheel hung with the souls of the damned and rotated with evident relish by Satan.

*Description*
Some early packs took the legend of King Midas who was awarded ass's ears by Apollo, after having given the judgement of a musical contest in favour of Pan, for their model of THE WHEEL OF FORTUNE. Four ass-eared figures are rotating around the wheel, with the inscriptions, 'I will rule. I have ruled. I am without rule. I rule'. Many Egyptian symbols were inserted during the reconstruction of the cards by such authorities as de Gebelin, Etteilla, Wirth and Waite, possibly because the wheel was used in Egyptian temples to denote the brevity of all human endeavour and the inconstancy of fortune. In some cards the wheel is set between two pillars, resting on leaves. A winged and crowned figure sitting at the top holing a cornucopia or horn of plenty, is menaced by a stealthy jackal or a fox. In others the Egyptian god Osiris sits at the top, or sometimes a sphinx, while on the rim the jackal-headed Anubis sits opposite Set, the Evil One, who is portrayed as a wolf. In other cards are found the four Holy Living Creatures found in Ezekiel, the lion, the eagle, the bull and Aquarius or man. Sometimes a serpent is found at the top of the wheel and the letters T.A.R.O. lettered around the hub interspersed with the letters for mercury, sulphur, salt and water

to correlate with the astrological symbols of the four holy figures.

*Symbolic Meaning*
Liberation from the round of incarnation, the gaining of wisdom and balance. The eternal process of evolution. The capriciousness of fate, the law of retribution of Karma, the unexpected twist of affairs that turns everything upside down.

*Actual Meaning*
'As ye sow so ye reap'. A new cycle in affairs. The solving of a problem through the progression of events. Destiny, success, good fortune, unexpected beneficial change, a reward of material wealth through past efforts.

*Reversed Meaning*
A slower and more difficult change, depending upon surrounding cards for rewards being fortunate or the opposite.

*Combinations*
If close to THE MAGICIAN, THE HERMIT, THE WORLD, or THE HIGH PRIESTESS, this is a very fortunate sign, and with THE CHARIOT this card means a great triumph. If followed, by THE MAGICIAN a happy and exciting change of profession, dwelling or direction in life. If THE MAGICIAN comes first the change will occur but later, and will bring success gradually. If THE HERMIT is near THE WHEEL this means light will be shed on hidden factors bringing success. THE WHEEL, when followed by THE HIGH PRIESTESS, means an artistic or scientific triumph, but if this order is reversed, the client has gifts he has not been able to develop, but through a new twist of fate will be able to do so, leading to great satisfaction and achievement.

## CARD NUMBER ELEVEN

## FORTITUDE: STRENGTH OR THE ENCHANTRESS

*Origin*

The origin of this figure is thought to be Cyrene. She was the handmaiden of Artemis, the moon goddess, who was seen by the Sun one day when she was wrestling barehanded with a lion. He became enamoured, and after obtaining the advice of a wise centaur he carried her off, mated with her and the result was a son, Aristaeus the huntsman god. Talismans using figures like that of FORTITUEDE were used to bind men to beasts, for ancient occultists believed that certain people possessed magical powers over the animal kingdom. The lion, the symbol of the sun or the masculine principle, was often coupled in magical lore with the unicorn, that fabled animal symbol of virginity and the moon.

*Description*

The early Minchiate packs showed a female Samson-like figure breaking a Grecian column in two with apparent ease. Others depicted a man clubbing a lion to death, this perhaps deriving from the legend of the labours of Hercules and linked again with the sun.

A young woman, sometimes depicted wearing a hat, or with the cosmic lemniscate over her head, with no apparent effort and evincing no fear whatsoever, is either opening or closing the jaws of a rather sleepy looking lion. Sometimes she wears a crown instead of the hat and sometimes wears roses in her hair and around her waist. The rose is said to symbolize the invincible union of desires and spiritual strength.

*Symbolic Meaning*

The moral force of purity which subdues passions and baser desires. The triumph of the spirit over the material world. The triumph of love over hate, of the positive forces over the negative, sacred love over profane.

*Actual Meaning*
Self discipline, strength and endurance, events overcome by will-power, moral victory, tolerance overcoming prejudice, mastery of circumstances, mastery of life, 'right is might'. Opportunity to put plans into action if the client has the courage to risk it. 'Stand fast, take courage.' The mind's domination over material adversities.

*Reversed Meaning*
There is no reversed meaning for FORTITUDE as this card dominates the other Major Arcana appearing with it and always remains the same. It is a very fortunate card indeed!

*Combinations*
This card is very strong and influences the whole of the layout. When followed by DEATH, it means an illness, serious but not fatal. When DEATH precedes FORTITUDE this means an abrupt ending of some matter; if both these cards are reversed, a narrow escape from injury and death. If FORTITUDE comes before THE CHARIOT, there will be a triumph after considerable effort. If THE CHARIOT comes first, this means great strength in future trials.

## CARD NUMBER TWELVE

## THE HANGED MAN

*Origin*
Thought to derive directly from the Orphic mystery rites and the worship of Dionysus, this card is said to depict sacrifice in order

to achieve regeneration. This has a corollary in the stories of Jesus, Odin and Osiris. In ancient times many images of Dionysus were hung in trees to ensure fertility. The death of the old year in pagan Britain was symbolized by the stoning of an effigy of Jack o'Lent or the Lord of Misrule. The Saturnalia and the Winter Carnival are derivatory of these beliefs. Mediaeval artists often depicted THE HANGED MAN as Judas Iscariot, bound or 'baffled' by the heels, which was the punishment meted out to criminals and debtors, and show the thirty pieces of silver falling from his pockets. The eighteenth-century occultists showed a semi-feminine youth posed erect, one foot loosely attached to a stake in the ground. The Rosicrucian school considered this card to mean the adept bound by his own engagements.

*Description*

The hanging figure seems peculiarly placid and at his ease, although suspended upside down, almost as if he is in a trance. He is suspended from his left foot on a rough gallows that is made from trees, and there are six branches either side. His arms form a triangle and his legs a cross. He is shown in some cards with only one shoe, and in some flowers bloom at the foot of the gibbet. Some cards depict him with a halo of light around his head, while others show coins falling from his pockets.

*Symbolic Meaning*

This card symbolizes a sacrifice, uncomplaining but entailing some suffering and hardship. It also means the complete reversal of a way of life; the changing of the natural order by a strong spiritual force. The falling coins are thought to portray a contempt for worldly riches.

*Actual Meaning*

Spiritual decision bringing serenity, wisdom, initiation, divination, intuition, suspended decisions, self-sacrifice, the gaining of inward peace and wisdom, occult prophetic power. Not always a happy card, for depending upon the surrounding cards, it can denote renunciation, destruction and abandonment.

*Reversed Meaning*

Vague idealism, futile sacrifice, selfishness, self absorption, hypocrisy, hidden plans, love of material things, false prophecy, arrogance, dependence upon the physical world: sometimes it can denote a death.

*Combinations*

THE HANGED MAN and TEMPERANCE together means hypocrisy of false promises bringing indecision. THE HANGED MAN and DEATH always mean a violent or unhappy demise or a matter involving sacrifice. If THE HANGED MAN precedes THE DEVIL, a great sacrifice will bring strength and power. THE DEVIL following THE HANGED MAN often refers to a combination, a partnership or marriage and shows that one or both of the partners will have to be prepared to give more.

## CARD NUMBER THIRTEEN

## DEATH

*Origin*

The origin of this card could be Moros, as the Greeks knew him. Mightier even than Zeus, he was the arbiter of Supreme Destiny. As did the Moire, he had three faces, Thanatos and Ked being the other two aspects, both pertaining to death. He is pictured here as the alter ego of Saturn, or time, waiting for no one, making no distinction between ruler and ruled. The original placement of this card was not number thirteen but was changed possibly because of the occult theory of numbers, based on the

Qabbala. Most modern occultists, influenced by the probably Shamanic origin of the Tarot, now consider this card to mean not death but transformation or a stripping away of all the base metals to reveal the gold beneath.

*Description*

In some packs this card is shown as a skeleton reaping a harvest of heads, arms and bones. One pack shows heads of children and heads wearing crowns. Waite's pack portrays a solemn knight carrying a banner emblazoned with the rose of life. He is mounted upon a beautiful white horse, riding across a countryside upon which the sun beams from between two towers. In the distance mountains and water can be seen. In front of him, women and children fall powerlessly while a bishop eagerly awaits his coming, face radiant, hands outstretched in welcome.

*Symbolic Meaning*

A deeply spiritual card, meaning the casting off of the material and the transformation and regeneration of the soul. It does not mean death, necessarily, but can have a ruthless, sudden and almost shocking connotation of death of the old life and the rebirth of the soul. It stands for change, and can sometimes bring with it shock and destruction prior to rebirth. This sometimes means that the change is in the consciousness of the individual or can denote artistic work of some importance being created after a struggle, or a new way of life leading to creative activity.

*Actual Meaning*

This card, in older readings, used to mean death of kings. It means the end of something prior to a change, destruction leading to transformation, change in consciousness. If badly aspected it can mean shocks and illness or all pretensions stripped away.

*Reversed Meaning*

Mortality, death or preoccupation with death. The lingering

effects of death of a loved one. Wilful destiny. Stagnation and boredom. An enforced removal of something which should have been given up voluntarily.

*Combinations*
With THE FALLING TOWER, this means a national disaster. However, if THE FALLING TOWER is reversed, and DEATH upright then there will be narrow escapes for calamity. DEATH preceding THE WORLD means that a world leader will die or there will be a world wide epidemic. DEATH followed by THE LOVERS, means the end of a marriage or a romance. When DEATH is inverted the marriage will be broken by death.

## CARD NUMBER FOURTEEN

## TEMPERANCE

*Origin*
This card may derive from Aquarius the Water Carrier, or perhaps Ganymede, the young prince of Troy who was abducted by Zeus to become the cupbearer of the gods and whose duty it was to refill the cup with the nectar of immortality whenever it became empty. The Egyptians always portrayed Aquarius with two vessels of water, and he, in turn, they identified with the god of the Nile, whose waters fed the lands in both a spiritual and a material sense. It has also been noted that mixing the water and wine was an ancient rite connected with Dionysus as his alter-ego Bacchus, and some Gnostic sects used two chalices to celebrate the Eucharist.

*Description*
In some packs this card is known as THE ANGEL OF TIME. It does

not refer to temperance as we use it in the more modern sense, but more in a modifying, mitigating sense. It shows a winged angel or female figure in long flowing robes wearing either a solar sign or a flower on her forehead, pouring out liquid in a shining stream from a chalice in her right hand to a chalice in her left. One foot is placed upon the earth and one in the water in some packs. Usually mountain peaks are depicted in the distance. Some show a shining sun rising above these, and flower and vegetation bloom at her feet.

*Symbolic Meaning*

The mountain peaks in the background are said to symbolize wisdom and understanding, while the pouring of the liquid from one vessel into another is said to denote the descent of spirit into matter, or the purifying of the soul by spiritual grace. The liquid is thought to be the stuff of the mind, the spiritual food acting upon the materially minded to give inspiration. It is considered by others, coming after DEATH, the transformation card, to denote an oblation to the gods, the cleansing and strenthening of the new soul. It signifies the combination of active and passive forces, the unifying of the male and female elements, and the stream that is shown in one pack, in which an angel is standing, is said to represent the past, present and future.

*Actual Meaning*

Moderation, economy, successful combinations, adaptation, consolidation, concession towards a common goal, stalemate before synthesis. Success through good management, life, vitality spiritual awareness and joy. It often means a rich marriage.

*Reversed Meaning*

This card annuls any vaccilation or indecisiveness, ill-advised partnerships, clashing interests, clumsy handling of potential.

*Combinations*

TEMPERANCE preceding JUSTICE means a long legal process resulting in equity and justice. If JUSTICE comes first, there will be delays and the matter may not eventuate. However when TEMPERANCE is inverted near this card, it puts an end to vacillation and hesitation. When with THE LOVERS this means indecision, hesitation, and deceit on the part of a lover.

## CARD NUMBER FIFTEEN

## THE DEVIL

*Origin*

The origin of this card is possibly Saturn once again. A figure very similar to this mediaeval concept of Satan was worshipped by the Knights Templar in a cult which appears to have been an off-shoot of Mithras, the Roman warrior god, equated with Dionysus, when the two cults blended together. They worshipped the unconquered sun, whose birthday every year on December 25th was celebrated by the slaying of a bull whose blood was sprinkled over the soil, to defeat the god of darkness. This links with Saturn, the death of winter and the rebirth of the sun. The Bahoment or Baphomet, a word derived from Mahommed, simply meaning idol, was often carved to represent an old bearded man, sometimes with two or three faces, and glowing eyes. This was derived from Janus, the guider of destinies and god of doorways and beginnings. Sometimes these idols have a cat's head, sometimes horns or birds' claws, sometimes cloven hoofs, sometimes wings sprouting from the shoulders, and cords or serpents binding the body. All these were connected with the worship of Satan. Christians thought this figure was Satan, and the Templars were accused of Devil worship and black magic.

Some modern packs still show the horns, the eagles' claws, the cloven hoofs and the cards or chains, while others portray the figure wearing a shamanic helmet and bats' wings. Levi changed the face of this card, for the earlier cards were not particularly evil in aspect but more mischievous.

*Description*

This card is sometimes called THE BLACK MAGICIAN. The figure, reminiscent of the mediaeval concept of Satan, stands on a box or pedestal from which chains loop out to imprison two smaller figures. His hands are in the reverse position of those of THE MAGICIAN whose opposite he is thought to represent. In some packs he holds a flaming torch upright in his left hand, in others he points a torch downwards in his right hand. In others, he holds a two-edged sword. In one Italian pack he is given horns, bat-like wings and a beard, like the Goat of Mendes. In the Marseilles pack he has wings and wears a shaman-like helmet, and has eagles' claws for feet. In the more esoteric cards, he wears the pentagram inverted between his horns, designating the black magician, and has claw-like feet. In versions based on Papus the smaller imps are depicted as a man and woman whose chains do not seem to be very tight, suggesting that mental strength could conquer fear and superstition and set them free. These are said by some to be the debased and bestialized version of THE LOVERS.

*Symbolic Meaning*

Man's bondage to evil through ignorance, fear and superstition. The symbol of materialism and domination of the physical, and the card of carnal desire. Revolutionary forces, violence and lack of sensitivity. Enormous power and effort used for destructive ends. The power of negative influences.

*Actual Meaning*

Unavoidable event, the outcome of which will depend upon surrounding cards. A temptation which if resisted will bring success. Unscrupulous domination of another person. Illness, violence, wealth obtained by dishonest means.

*Reversed Meaning*
Spiritual healing and protection in a potentially dangerous situation. Illness averted or healed. Punishment. Even when reversed this card brings a suggestion of an almost irresistible moral force that brings destruction and suffering, and which very few people would be strong enough to resist.

*Combinations*
When THE EMPEROR appears with THE DEVIL and THE DEVIL comes first, then there will be anarchy and agitation on a national scale. If THE EMPEROR comes first, particularly if THE DEVIL is reversed, either a national figure is threatened with evil or alien forces or a powerful and upstanding person will be ruined by a scandal or evil forces, working against him. If preceding JUSTICE there will be a miscarriage of justice and if coming after JUSTICE an accusation will be proved false. If THE POPE comes with THE DEVIL they almost cancel each other out, however it depends if THE DEVIL comes first, for this card has the greater power. But the outcome will depend upon the surrounding cards.

## CARD NUMBER SIXTEEN

## THE FALLING TOWER OR THE LIGHTNING-STRUCK TOWER

*Origin*
The origin of this card is thought to lie in the rites of the Dionysian cult which was linked with that of Mithras. The Titans tore Dionysian to pieces and were blasted by divine lightning, then

Dionysus arose like the Phoenix reborn from the ashes in the new personality of Iacchus. The same force which destroyed the Titans regenerated Dionysus. The power of enlightened good has defeated the power of ignorance, and evil; or, winter is dead, a world is reborn, a new god arises.

*Description*

Early Italian decks referred to this card as THE CASTLE OF PLUTO, god of the underworld. Some old French packs called it LE MAISON DIEU but as this word derived from diefel (the Devil) it had a similar meaning to the Italian pack. Another name was L'HOPITAL or hospes, meaning an inn or hostelry, while another, showing a giant arrow of lightning striking and destroying battlements, was called LA SAGITTA. To some early Christians this card represented Sodom and Gomorrah, and some said the people falling from the edifice were Nimrod and his ministers falling from the tower of Babel.

The card shows a tower struck by a lightning bolt, apparently emanating from a sunny blue sky. Figures are falling out of small windows and the tower, which has a turreted top, is swaying, just about to collapse. Sometimes a woman is shown outside the tower weeping. On most cards a shower of bricks and masonry is seen, on others the drops of condensation which some scholars assert are Hebrew Yods, the symbols of spiritual matter descending into the material world. The Marseilles pack shows a feathery red-golden lightning bolt striking the crenellated tower, which is surrounded by shapes that look like cannon balls floating in the air.

*Symbolic Meaning*

The card of catastrophe and sudden change, depending upon the surroundings cards, it carries the connotation of liberation of the flesh, the end of the Karmic circle, the stopping of the wheel, the darkness illuminated by spirit and knowledge. The sun shining could mean divine enlightenment and the shattering of illusions and dreams in order to build a more permanent life foundation. It symbolizes the overthrow of governments and systems and a cleansing catharsis.

*Actual Meaning*
Unexpected shock or catastrophe, liberation from restrictions, disruption that will bring eventual happiness, selfish people brought to their knees, a change of life pattern, traditions challenged, misguided selfish ambitions shattered, bankruptcy, the coming of enlightenment.

*Reversed Meaning*
This card is actually stronger when reversed, meaning oppression, conflict, self-undoing, obstacles, domination, imprisonment and a disaster which could have been avoided. Beneficial results will be longer in coming or in being apparent after a catastrophe.

*Combinations*
When preceding THE HIGH PRIESTESS, this means disaster in the sphere of religion or in a traditionally established institution. When these cards are reversed, it usually means injuries to the brain, a mental breakdown and consequent physical collapse.

## CARD NUMBER SEVENTEEN

## THE STAR

*Origin*
The star pictured in this card may be Hesperus or Venus, the lode star of the ancients. The Greeks had two names for it, for they saw it at two different times, once after sunset, when it was

called Hesperus Aster, and once as the herald of the dawn, when it was called Phosphorous Aster. The reborn Dionysus, Iacchus, was known as Phosphorus Aster. The card could also be identified with the Sumerian goddess Innana or Astarte, as she later became, who every year on the festival day of the god Adonis was summoned by the light of the morning star to waken this Dionysus of the east from his tomb. One authority suggests that the background of water, trees and flowers could pertain to the scenery of the old Greek mystery plays, while another thinks that the pool could represent the two pools in the underworld, or memory and forgetfulness. This pool, then, would be the pool of memory from which the initiate would drink so as to always remember his mystical experience.

*Description*

The Minchiate pack depicts the three Magi following the star of Bethlehem. The Marseilles pack shows a beautiful nude maiden kneeling by a stream or pool, pouring two pitchers or vessels, into the water in front of her. Above her burns a bright star, surrounded by a constellation of smaller stars. This set features the eight pointed star of Innana but other packs use the five pointed magical device, known as the pentacle or the star of Solomon. In some cards the kneeling maiden has one foot in the water and one on land. In other cards, there is no pool, and she appears to be pouring the liquid on to the earth. On most cards, an ibis is seen, or a bird in a tree, in some a butterfly on a flower, or a lotus blossom. Both the butterfly and the ibis symbolized the soul in Egyptian belief and the lotus was sacred to them. Above the kneeling figure, the seven smaller stars are thought to be the Pleiades while the large pure star shining over her head is said to represent cosmic light and energy. However, the earliest cards showed only seven stars in all.

*Symbolic Meaning*

The symbol of beautiful and eternal youth, the maiden pours the waters of life onto the land, the material world, and into the stream, the universal consciousness of mind and spirit. She symbolizes refreshment, hope and love, life after death, spiritual love and inspiration, renewal and encouragement through unselfish aid.

*Actual Meaning*
Renewed effort brings attainment; good health and loving friends; courage, inspiration, spiritual strength, love of humanity, hope and optimism, gifts from unselfish friends, firm promises, keeping faith strong and looking upwards.

*Reversed Meaning*
False hope and false promises, negative thinking, delays and doubt, refusal to change, pessimism, intolerant attitudes.

*Combinations*
If THE STAR precedes THE EMPRESS it denotes a happy, ordered and tranquil existence. If THE MAGICIAN follows THE STAR this augurs a happy beginning for a new project or artistic venture. If THE EMPRESS comes before this card there will be assured success through strong ambition and effort.

## CARD NUMBER EIGHTEEN

### THE MOON

*Origin*
This is Diana, the huntress and goddess of the moon, with two of her hounds who are thought to be guarding the portals of the underworld. Some scholars seem to think the two pillars represent the Pillars of Hercules, those twin portals that the Ancients

believed guarded not only the Straits of Gibraltar but also the entrance to the underworld. We have also the concept of the two pillars of Boaz and Jakin, as mentioned before, and also the drops of condensation being Hebrew Yods. The original creature portrayed as rising from the pond was a crab, which in astrological lore is governed by the moon. The pool is depicted possibly because the moon also runs the sea and tides, all aquatic creatures and all reflecting surfaces, and was itself considered to be a mirror. A talisman from *The Picatrix* thought to bring fertility, protect women and children, calm the emotions and strangely enough act as an antidote to poison, was made when the moon was in the first degree of Cancer and showed a woman riding a crab-like creature and holding a mirror in her hand. In some cards, a scroll is seen with the word Ma printed on it, which has led one student of the Tarot to claim a connection between the Tarot and the lost continent of Mu.

*Description*

Some early decks show the goddess Diana holding a crescent moon, or as in the eighteenth century packs, a waning moon. Etteilla's design showed a full moon surrounded by stars, but modern authorities usually portray the moon in all three aspects so as to give the fuller meaning. Other packs portrayed two astrologers busily engaged in measuring the ascension of the moon, and an Italian pack illustrated the effect of the moon's rays, by depicting a lover serenading his sweetheart beneath her balcony. A card of three levels, emotional, mental and spiritual, the moon is shown with all three faces in evidence. The dogs are derivative of Hecate, goddess of the dark moon, whose power encompassed hell, heaven and earth, linking again with the three levels of this card. The moon is shown, with all three faces shining down from between two pillars or turreted forts, upon a pool from which is struggling a crab-like creature. Above the pool stand two dogs, or a dog and a wolf, whose heads are raised and jaws open as they bay to their goddess. Dew drops or condensation fall from the moon onto the grass and plants growing around the pool.

*Symbolic Meaning*
The moon is said by some occultists to represent the reflected light of the subconscious, the dream world and the imagination. It is symbolic of intuition, hallucination, dreams, occult forces, and fluctuations.

*Actual Meaning*
It can be unfortunate, depending upon the other surrounding cards and can mean a crisis of faith, fluctuation in affairs, intuition, self deception, secret enemies, deception from others, hidden spite and envy, danger and trouble to loved ones.

*Reversed Meaning*
This weakens the card. It could mean the harnessing of the imagination for profit, or peace gained after an enormous effort, or a Pyrrhic victory; a failure of nerve, fear of the unfamiliar. It has the connotation of 'take what you want, the good God says, but pay for it'.

*Combinations*
When near THE FALLING TOWER, THE DEVIL, DEATH or JUSTICE, this card has a strong malign influence. If JUSTICE comes first it can denote slander and unjust accusation, and if DEATH is close it could mean a suicide as a result of slander. Only if both cards are reversed will the power be weakened and truth discovered, averting all harm. When THE MOON precedes THE FALLING TOWER, fraud, deceit, and self deception bring ruin and disgrace. THE MOON, if in front of THE LOVERS, means the end of a love affair through deception or lies. Or it can mean the illusion of love which comes to an abrupt end.

## CARD NUMBER NINETEEN

### THE SUN

*Origin*

The celestial master to the initiate in the mysteries; to the ordinary person, the sun brought warmth, joy, laughter and abundance. The ancient talisman for success showed a crowned king triumphant, similar to that of THE EMPEROR trump, either driving a chariot or sitting on a throne with a celestial globe beneath the feet. To many of the Ancients the sun was a symbol of kingship and royalty. The ancient Romans and Egyptians used it to decorate their buildings, their rulers used it in their devices, and the ordinary folk carried talismans for protection and success. This card many have a link with Phaeton who drove the celestial carriage through the heavens and lost control, and was himself destroyed by fire. The sun's birthday was at the winter solstice, on December 25th, a date which was officially adopted by the Christian church as the birthday of Christ, to facilitate teaching and conversion. Fire was considered to be purifying and a protection against evil and as always considered to be connected with the sun. Bonfires were lit for purification purposes, and people and animals passed through them, but the most magical and sacred were the elf fires, those which happened spontaneously as a result of the concentration of the sun's rays, and were thought to be a powerful protection against evil.

*Description*

In the older Tarot packs children are depicted running or playing beneath the sun. In the Minchiate, the children have become young lovers. Some early packs showed a spinner spinning or unwinding thread, The Waite pack depicts a joyous child astride a white horse, flourishing a large banner. There are the ever familiar dew drops which de Gebelin described as 'tears of pearl and gold'. In all cards the sun beams down, rayed with light and dropping dew onto two children who stand in front of a low stone wall. The children are sometimes dancing, the sky is shining blue, there are sunflowers peeping over the wall and the card emanates a radiant happiness and triumph.

*Symbolic Meaning*

This card symbolizes the end of self deception, the bright warm light of day, innocence, purity, strength and courage, the conquering regenerative force and positive thinking.

*Actual Meaning*

Triumph and achievement in any field, particularly in art and science. Happy meetings, a wealthy marriage, liberation from routine, gratitude, for life's gifts, material happiness, the realization of ambition, protection, studies completed, health, joy and success against all odds, pleasure in simple things.

*Reversed Meaning*

This card, although weakened when reversed, still retains its essential meaning.

*Combinations*

If this card precedes DEATH, there will be a triumph, through something being finished, ending or dying. A death will bring benefit or vindication. When with THE FALLING TOWER, out of evil comes good, so a sudden catastrophe proves of ultimate benefit.

## CARD NUMBER TWENTY

## JUDGEMENT

*Origin*
This card possibly has for its central figure St Michael, one of the seven Archangels who are said to be responsible for keeping the planets on their courses. Hermes and Michael have a function in common, for Michael guides the souls into the new world and Mercury was the guide to the souls in the underworld. This card has the connotation of reincarnation rather than the Christian concept of judgement for past sins and then rebirth.

*Description*
Some packs depict God among his angels. In the Etteilla pack there was no angel, and Papus conceived a rather sentimental card showing mother, father and child at the resurrection. Most later packs depict an angel blowing a trumpet from which hangs the cross of St Michael, over graves that are opening revealing naked figures with their arms stretched upwards. Sometimes the mountains are portrayed in the distance. Quite a number of older packs called this card THE ANGEL.

*Symbolic Meaning*
This card is the symbol of the eternal spirit, the cycle of birth in death, the end and the beginning of an existence, the Karmic round.

*Actual Meaning*
Resolution and completion. A mental awakening that could precede fame and success. Justified pleasure in achievement. Change and renewal, a beneficial influence, a new lease of life. The final outcome. A summing up.

*Reversed Meaning*
A highly spiritual card, this card loses its strength when surrounded by physical cards such as THE WHEEL OF FORTUNE, THE DEVIL, OR THE MAGICIAN. When reversed but not in company with any of these it means impermanent fame or transient success, loss of health or material possessions, bitterness or weakness, fear of death, or fear and bitterness in old age.

*Combinations*
This card is a very powerful card so when combined with THE CHARIOT it means fame and triumph. If reversed, the meaning is reversed too. If JUDGEMENT comes before THE CHARIOT reversed, it means the triumph will be short lived, for the effect of the sudden success will weaken the character. If THE HERMIT follows this card, triumph will always be of an inner spiritual kind, or will only be apparent after death. If THE HERMIT is reversed, there will be discoveries of great benefit made public.

## CARD NUMBER TWENTY-ONE

## THE WORLD

*Origin*
This trump is said to be derived directly from the Greek mysteries, and depicts the culmination of the rites, when the initiate, having successfully passed through his ordeals, is dressed in honour of the sun and presented to the populace. Indeed, Aupelius describes in detail his graduation at the conclusion of the rites, in *The Golden Ass*, and furnishes us with a description of the garments he wore. They consisted of a flower-embroidered robe and a long floating scarf called an olympian stole, while he carried a torch in one hand and a palm chaplet with leaves sticking out like the rays of the sun in the other. The early

French packs titled this card THE CARD OF THE MAGI and it is not surprising that it is considered to be the best card in the pack, and carries the meaning of completion and reward.

*Description*

The old Visconti pack shows two cherubs supporting a globe containing towers that rise from the sea under the light of glittering stars. The picture is surrounded by a wreath or garland and in each corner are the familiar four living creatures found in Ezekiel, which also stood for the four cardinal elements and the four directions. In the more modern Tarots, a dancing female figure is shown, with left leg crossed behind her, a direct contrast to THE HANGING MAN. Sometimes she carries a mirror in her hand, or a rod, or two rods, one in both hands, and occasionally she is depicted holding a crown. She is partially draped with a gracefully floating stole, and is pictured inside an oval Mandala or wreath, bound in four places by ribbon or roses. In each corner are the four living creatures.

*Symbolic Meaning*

The dancer denotes joy and happiness, the mirror derives from the Sistrum of Isis, the wreath and the crown denote joyous celebration and the attainment of the initiate who has mastered the truth. Levi says this garland, symbolizing truth, is less easily broken than chains of iron. It is the culmination of the entire series and represents finality, the final completion of the cycle which commenced with THE MAGICIAN, and led through triumphs, temptations, snares and new experiences, and entailed the casting off of the baser self, the discarding of false illusion and the finding of truth. It denotes the birth of a new being through the merging of consciousness with super-consciousness. This is the summing up, the reward for lessons well learned.

*Actual Meaning*

The seeker of perfection, the attainment of great success, material and spiritual. The occult, material or spiritual triumph, and reward. The lesson learned, individually perfected happiness, joy, celebration, movement, travel over water or across the world, a triumphant conclusion to a matter, or the end of a cycle.

*Reversed Meaning*
A person who is in a rut; the sacrifice of love for material considerations, fear of change, refusal to learn the lessons of life, over-attachment to possessions and surroundings, the fear of the unknown, failure of the Will, stagnation.

*Combinations*
If this card is combined with THE SUN it brings a wonderful emotional experience, or joy, love and harmony. If it comes after THE HANGED MAN it denotes that a loving sacrifice will bring a triumph. If THE WORLD comes first, it means a sacrifice that could bring sadness and parting.

## UNNUMBERED CARD OR 'O'

## THE FOOL

*Origin*
This card, sometimes at the beginning and sometimes at the end of the pack is the derivation of our modern Joker and one of the most significant cards in the series. THE FOOL or THE JESTER as he is known is direct descendant of the old 'Lord of Misrule' and of Dionysus himself. The amalgamation of Mithras and Dionysus brought with it a number of feasts and festive rites, the principal feasts of which were the Saturnalia. Only two remain today – Holy Innocents' Day and Christmas Day. On Holy Innocent's day, the Lord of Misrule, or Dionysus in revolt, traditionally

threw over the established rule and rebelled against the restrictions of authority as a symbol of his search for spiritual enlightenment and rebirth. His descendant THE FOOL, the eternal scapegoat, played an important part in mediaeval feudal society, and the motley and bells became an honoured and respected symbol of service. The jester's cap is thought to derive from the horns or asses' ears worn by Dionysus and early packs feature a type of horned jester's cap, and others show him clad in motley, and carrying a bladder and bells.

*Description*

His is portrayed in gay clothing, stepping out carelessly sometimes with either a dog or a dragon snapping at his heels, a small bundle tied to to the end of a stick across his shoulders. In some cards he carries a staff, in others he flourishes a white rose, and in most designs it appears he is just about to step off a precipice of which he seems unaware. Some early packs portrayed him as a penitential beggar clad in white, wandering the highways of life; others clad him in tattered rags.

*Symbolic Meaning*

Some authorities claim that the crocodile, considered by the Egyptians as the sacred and all-seeing, which is often portrayed at his heels denotes that THE FOOL is possessed of divine wisdom, and that he is ignoring the national world and commencing the journey of life,armed with a spiritual strength which will protect him from all physical dangers. He is the Eternal Traveller about to undergo any of the experiences of life in order to learn its secrets. He must make his choices, abandon, adopt, embrace or discard in order to attain perfection. Some early moralists, writing about this card, considered that the bundle or purse he carries contains all the sins and vices of the world.

*Actual Meaning*

A choice of vital importance needing great wisdom. 'Divine discontent'. The seeker of experiences, spiritually guided. The blithe spirit. Nevertheless, it also carries the elements, of anarchy, the irrational human element, the unexpected, the breakdown of the existing order for the materialist, light-heartedness, heedlessness, recklessness and travel.

*Reversed Meaning*
A faulty choice or impediment to progress.

*Combinations*
This card being a highly spiritual card, it combines only with those on the same plane and is cancelled out by some powerful material cards such as THE WHEEL OF THE DEVIL. If this card follows THE HERMIT a secret will come to light and be aired for discussion. If the other way around a secret is now safe. THE FOOL with THE CHARIOT denotes important news and THE FOOL and THE SUN mean something unexpected will occur that will bring order, comfort and happiness.

*Chapter Four*

# Some General Points

## COMBINATIONS OF THE MAJOR ARCANA

Sometimes, when one strong card is inverted and precedes another strong card which is upright, one neutralizes the other. For instance THE EMPRESS and THE DEVIL; THE DEVIL and THE STAR; THE SUN and THE TOWER; all these cancel each other out.

JUSTICE which is a physical card, cannot combine with THE EMPRESS, nor does it combine well with THE WORLD, for THE WORLD is essentially an abstract card. THE HERMIT and THE WORLD are incompatible too, for THE HERMIT's symbology is too narrow to combine with that of THE WORLD. This also applies to THE MAGICIAN and THE WORLD. When JUSTICE comes before THE HANGED MAN it shows that clemency and tolerance should be shown rather than cold hard judgement. JUDGEMENT is a spiritual card, and concerned with intellectual matters, so it does not combine well with such physical cards as THE WHEEL OF FORTUNE or THE DEVIL. THE DEVIL is a card of events which must follow inexorably to a conclusion.

THE HIGH PRIESTESS gives self awareness and depth of meaning to all the other cards surrounding her, and often shows new avenues and opportunities for advancement.

FORCE is one of the strongest cards in the pack and sets the tone for the entire reading. It destroys THE STAR and even dominates THE DEVIL. Another card which influences every other card in the pack is THE TOWER. THE WORLD is the only card which can mitigate its influence, by making the outcome general rather than particular, as in a world scale misfortune such as an epidemic or a universal disaster. FORCE however would increase its potency and THE DEVIL its darker aspect.

*Pairings and Trios*

If there is a preponderance of the Major Arcana in the reading then destiny is taking a hand in the client's life and the events will be out of his control. If the cards seem to favour one suit, such as Wands, then the accent of the reading will be on career and business; if Cups, then love affairs and social life will predominate; if Pentacles, then money affairs would dominate the reading; and if Spades, the reading would contain much predicted turbulence, spiritual suffering and perhaps illness. If the court cards are all of the same suit the same emphasis would apply only more strongly, so that if all the court cards were of the Spades suit, the client would have a difficult time through envious and hostile enemies actively attacking him.

## THE MINOR ARCANA:

### Its Symbology and Meaning

There are four suits in the Minor Arcana: Swords, Cups, Pentacles, (they can be called Deniers) and Clubs which are also known as Staves or Wands in some packs. They were adapted by the French knight, de Vignoles (known as Lanire) in the fifteenth century for the game of Piquet – a game of chivalry – and his playing cards had carreaux or arrowheads, trefoils or clovers cups and piques, the points of the lances. From these come our modern packs, the Cups being our Hearts, the Carreaux or arrow heads our Diamonds, the Trefoils or clovers our Clubs and the Piquet or lance points, our Spades. The Tarot court, or 'coat' cards as they were first known, include a Knave or Servitor as well as the Knight (our Jack) and the King and Queen. Often in the early cards the servitor or knave was depicted as a maid of honour, (the name 'knave' simply meant 'son') and these cards can mean either sex. Possibly the entourage was the representation of a feudal court of mediaeval family.

The suit of Swords covers all things connected with spiritual stress, struggle, strife, battle, loss and worry, trials, competition, and always loneliness of spirit. The suit of Cups pertains to all things connected with love, joyous fulfilment, procreation, home, success, friendship and human relationships. The suit of Clubs rules all things concerned with the lasting values, such as serenity, security both emotional and material, artistic endeavour, talents, careers, contracts and agreements in business, new opportunity, deep sea travel and artistic triumphs and expansion. The suit of Deniers or Pentacles refers to financial transactions, material gain, windfalls, the inheritance of unearned money, legal matters pertaining to money and all things material but impermanent.

## THE SUIT OF CUPS

Pertaining to love, success, happiness, protection, social matters, abundance.

KING. A professional man, in the Church or connected with law, he is warm hearted, sympathetic, sensitive and creative, and a good husband. This man is a man of ideas, skilled in the ways of the world. He always looks after himself first. He can represent a negotiator in favour of the client.

QUEEN. The loved one or mistress, she is a highly artistic woman, romantic, slightly fey and prophetic, very sensitive and a visionary. This card can also mean a good mixer, love and a happy marriage.

KNIGHT. A single, young bachelor, he is a refined, artistic, high-principled man and may be a lover, a seducer or a rival in love. He can also denote a pleasant visit or a proposition, a message, advances, an invitation, or the bearer of a message.

KNAVE. News, a message, the birth of a child, new methods in business, a willing and a helpful youth who gives good advice or is of a quiet, artistic and meditative nature are all shown by this card.

ACE. The Ace means passion, inspiration, love, joy, and spiritual nourishment, replenishment. It can mean love, marriage and motherhood. This is the card of feminine gestation of the Minor Arcana signifying faith, fruitful abundance, creative talent, enterprise in creation, good news, gay company. When near the love cards this means either true love or great rewards from a loving union.

TWO. The two means partnership, loving union, friendship, the reconciliation of opposites, the resolution of quarrels, the end of rivalry, the signing of a contract or treaty, and wealth, but restriction.

THREE. Emotional growth, liaison, a love affair, happiness and fulfilment in marriage, fruition, maternity, comfort, trust, happy issue, conclusion of a happy matter, a healing of wounds, congratulations and rejoicing are all shown by the Three.

FOUR. The Four reveals outside meddling in matters of the heart, hostile influence, discontent with prevailing circumstances and environment leading to a fresh evaluation of material success and a seeking of new paths. The 'divine discontent' card – when badly aspected this card means boredom, and also timidity in pursuing new paths.

FIVE. Inheritance, gifts, an old life finished, something lost – this card means regret for a wrong choice or past actions, new alternatives to be explored when something is lost or finished, disappointment in marriage, or a love affair gone wrong.

SIX. This is a card of conflict and reconciliation, the results of past action and influences evidencing themselves in the present. Sometimes begins now which has its roots in the past – past efforts bringing present rewards. An old friend or lover appears, or a long-held dream or a love affair with roots in the past is realized. When badly aspected this card means that the client lives too much in the past.

SEVEN. There is an exceptional choice to be made and much care and consideration must be given. Imagination, dreams, and mental activity are shown by this 'Castles in Spain' card, as are creative inspiration, mystical experience, the unexpected, a surprise to do with mental or creative activity. If badly aspected this person has too many interests and should settle to one main activity.

EIGHT. Leaving the past behind, new experiences, new friends, new activities, leaving a place or abandoning a situation, a change of attitude through disillusion or suffering, a person 'refined by the flame to rise like a phoenix': all these may be indicated by the Eight.

NINE. The 'wish card' signifies the total fulfilment of one paramount desire, as well as generosity, kindliness, good health and success, and stability both emotional and material.

TEN. This card, pertaining to property or a residence, also

means honour, fame, publicity and prestige, the love of friends, lasting success. It denotes work to do with the public, and also peace of mind and prosperity.

## THE SUIT OF STAVES, WANDS OR CLUBS

Pertaining to the professions, property, consolidation, the arts, new ventures, stability and success.

KING. A dark man, honest, upright, generous and strong, possibly a family man, he gives good impartial advice and sympathy. He also means successful business dealings and an unexpected heritage.

QUEEN. A woman of medium dark colouring of friendly, generous and tolerant disposition, a home and country lover, she is independent, protective and makes a good friend. She also means a successful business transaction and new enterprises.

KNIGHT. This card means a young man, medium dark, and is also the 'intuition card', as well as the card which can mean emigration. It denotes flight, change of residence, departure, also conflict and rivalry in business if badly aspected, and can sometimes mean good stable sense in money matters.

KNAVE. The Knave can be the bearer of a message from a loved one: a postman, a messenger, or an adaptable bright young person of either sex. He means good news, or stimulating news pertaining to finances. This card can also, when placed next to a male court card, mean honours or good news about a child.

ACE. The Ace indicates a new undertaking, also a new foundation for success, artistic inspiration, wisdom, innovation, creation, abundance, a new cycle of creative activity, the founding of a family, or the basis for founding a fortune.

TWO. Intellectual work, courage and initiative overcoming obstacles, high motives, tolerance, justice, wisdom, scientific men in a high place giving help, authority and success through strength and vision – the two of staves can be any of these.

THREE. Partnership brings wealth and fame. The Three can also signify enterprises, a good start, help from a powerful friend, original ideas, powerful convictions, good powers of expression, rewards from work of an inspirational nature, an artist or inventor who turns dreams into reality, a trade partnership, or efforts rewarded.

FOUR. The card of the successful designer or inventor it shows the professional realm of ideas allied to the beauty of perfected work, and also a pause in activities, a peaceful tranquil period away from the demands of society, romance, the family bond, harmony and the 'Harvest Home'.

FIVE. A struggle in love and in life is indicated: love triumphs over obstacles. Mental ability is needed to avoid defeat. It may mean overcoming obstacles, then a change for the better after the struggle.

SIX. The fulfilment of hopes and wishes in one's career, wonderful news, victory over a situation, diplomacy overcoming opposition, achievement and great satisfaction are shown by the six.

SEVEN. A successful change in profession is assured but strength and determination are needed to achieve success. Opposition is defeated through sustained effort and great courage. The Seven also signifies dissemination of knowledge, writing, lecturing, teaching: it is the 'teacher' card.

EIGHT. The Eight indicates the time to be up and doing something new, the end of a period of calm or the end of a delay, approaching a goal, taking a journey, haste in travel, movement, news coming quickly, overseas travel or overseas connections – and the arrows of love.

NINE. This card is better than the nine of cups, the 'wish card'; it is the strongest in the pack and brings a safe and unassailable position. It brings success particularly in the fields of the arts or the professions. It can denote advice given or taken, expansion, balanced judgement, honesty, integrity, courage in defence, strength in reserve and victory through strength and integrity.

TEN. The card of consolidation, it pertains to big business, new contracts, new ventures or an overseas journey or trip to a strange place. It can also mean a burden soon to be lifted, or a problem solved. Doing things the hard way – the end of narrow-minded fixed ideas.

## THE SUIT OF DENIERS OR PENTACLES

Pertaining to all money matters, litigation and material wealth.

KING. He indicates a fair man, possibly inarticulate and uneducated, but intuitive, patient, wise and loyal. He has a mathematical bent. Disinterested, he could be unsympathetic, has a slow, deliberate turn of mind, and is stable and cautious. He would make a good parent but a bad enemy.

QUEEN. A fair-headed woman, possibly of independent means, she is materialistic, practical and loves the good things in life. The card has the connotation of money-making, wealth and responsibility to wealth.

KNIGHT. A young man, he could be a new acquaintance, or could mean an indiscretion with the opposite sex. The young man is materialistic, leans to established forms of authority, is traditional, persevering and has a code of honour. This card can also mean the coming and going of a matter, or laborious work, and much patience needed to see it through.

KNAVE. This card can mean a message containing good news, or a letter with money in it. The knave is a young fair boy or girl, avaricious and materialistic, but diligent. This card also means respect for learning, new opinions, new ideas and scholarship.

ACE. The Ace can show the beginning of an enterprise that

will bring monetary reward. Gifts, legacies, the appreciation of beauty on a physical plane, materialistic comfort, gold, prosperity, luxury, love of possessions, sensuousness, endurance, stoicism, security based on a firm foundation – the Ace of Pentacles an signify all these.

TWO. The Two means fluctuations in fortune, the need for skilful manipulation to achieve success, imminent change, harmony in the midst of change, new moves, and news pertaining to journeys, communication, success in one direction, the use of one talent to achieve success, or gifts coming.

THREE. The Three can betoken professionalism and craftsmanship, success after training, or hard work and consistent effort. It can also indicate a good time for business expansion, skill in trade, artistry, success, help, co-operation, renown through ability, esteem, honour and glory.

FOUR. Possessions and material acquisitiveness are shown by the Four, as are obstacles and problems of financial nature, the establishment of a business or commercial firm, inheritance, a legacy – and miserly tendencies, if badly aspected.

FIVE. 'Needs must when the devil drives'. The head ruled by the heart brings sorrow: the Five can mean love gone astray, enforced restrictions, spiritual loneliness; if badly aspected, homesickness, loss of security or loss of position in life.

SIX. The theatrical or entertainment card of the Minor Arcana, it means help from above, or help from a generous person, just rewards, money affairs put on a stable footing, sympathy, kindness and charity. When unfavourably situated this means a lawsuit over money.

SEVEN. The Seven can signify a gift or sudden gain. 'Procrastination is the thief of time': it is a warning to work consistently, for past efforts will only be successful through consistent effort. It is the card of barter, loan and money, but with a possibility of delay. This card could also mean a potential suitor, or results from the past bearing fruit.

EIGHT. The Eight indicates a change that will bring material benefits. The 'talent card' allied with energy, it may presage turning skills into a profession or money earned through talent or skill, possible employment to come but in a new skilled field, beginning again, or the reward of labour.

NINE. A substantial income earned through effort and thrift and material wealth may be meant by the Nine. The reward for effort and sound administration, the successful completion of something resulting in rewards and comfort, and the solution to a problem are also possible meanings.

TEN. The ten covers everything pertaining to the house and family: a purchase or sale, establishing a family tradition, reverence for history, tradition and a settled way of life, money spent on a house, buying or selling, blood ties and inheritance, property concerns, dowries, and legacies.

## THE SUIT OF SWORDS

Pertaining to the struggles of the spirit, competition, battle, strife, striving and growing, and loneliness.

KING. Possibly a dark man of authority, or an intellectual with strong moral conviction, he can be a severe critic, and often is a legal man or counsellor. He could be an innovator, but is often found in government, the armed forces or the legal profession.

QUEEN. A woman possibly dark and often in authority, she is self-reliant and strong. This is the widow's card, and it carries with it a sense of sadness and privation. She makes a good friend but a bad enemy. This card also denotes the struggle of spirit over material concerns, or can denote attention to detail.

KNIGHT. A dark impetuous man or a mischief-maker of either sex may enter the client's life for good or ill. It also means a fighter, a person who is at his best in a difficult situation, or skill in defence and courage in struggle and combat. It can mean a struggle yet to come, or if near cards meaning illness can denote the surgeon.

KNAVE. This card can mean inner conflict which is the result of past injustices, possibly during childhood, an unscrupulous rival in business, or a deceitful person who carries tales, or spies; it can also mean scrutiny or a diplomatic messenger who will negotiate business.

ACE. The symbol of strength in adversity and triumph over great odds, it can be the sword of Damocles or the symbol of divine justice. Just rewards are indicated, or a sense of the inevitable, something which is beginning and which cannot be stopped, but will change the entire life. 'The old order changeth'. This is a card of great force for either good or ill, for love or hate. It means victory after conquest.

TWO. The stalemate: this is the card of balanced forces, meaning help and friendship in adversity, good coming out of evil, a sense of equilibrium. If badly aspected this card means impotence and indecision.

THREE. This card can mean a severing of ties, breaking up a partnership or marriage, a permanent or temporary separation. It always means disruption or upheaval, such as sorrow and tears over a faithless lover, but it always carries the sense of clearing the ground for something new, 'the darkest hour before the dawn'.

FOUR. A voluntary period of quiet is possible after a test or battle. It can also mean firm administration pertaining to law, peace and order after struggle and chaos, occultism, mediation, religion, rest. It can mean hospitalization and convalescence, or merely a period of quiet for thinking things through.

FIVE. The client must learn to accept the inevitable, acknowledge defeat and swallow false pride in order to build on more secure foundations, or proceed in a new direction. It can mean a narrow escape from physical danger, or a threat averted, but it usually denotes the acceptance of limitations before moving upwards and onwards.

SIX. This is the card of travel or flight, usually denoting a change to a more pleasing environment, or position. It also means success after worry or anxiety, or the removal of a large obstacle after a period of strain. It could also denote an overseas visitor or the taking of risks which would turn out favourably.

SEVEN. 'Softly softly catchee monkey' . . . this card denotes the necessity for prudence and evasion in order to gain an objective. The use of brain not brawn is indicated, and direct or aggressive tactics would be disastrous. It can denote partial success or uncertain hope, and possibly the danger of injury while travelling or when indulging in sport.

EIGHT. This is the card which means the bonds will soon be broken and the restrictions lifted, but patience and attention to detail will be needed to avoid criticism. Perhaps there is doubt as to which direction to take, but a sign will come to lead the way.

NINE. This card can mean a difficult choice entailing suffering and sacrifice or the death of a loved one, bringing sorrow and desolation, as well as patient suffering borne with fortitude. It can mean a road accident or loss, if badly aspected.

TEN. This card can be taken on two levels, the national and the personal. It can mean the lowest point in a nation's economy, or the lowest ebb of human affairs. It can also denote self-honesty, the beginnings of seeing a dream, infatuation, relationship or illusion for what it's really worth; it can, if badly aspected, mean sudden misfortune, pain and even ruin and if near JUSTICE and THE DEVIL can denote imprisonment. But on a spiritual plane it can mean the end of the darkness and the beginning of light.

## SOME DIFFERENT COMBINATIONS OF THE MINOR ARCANA

FOUR ACES. A favourable chance leads to a new life.
THREE ACES. Artistic success comes with something new.
TWO ACES. If red, marriage; if black, a new project or contracts are to be expected.
FOUR KINGS. This means a great honour, and often public acclaim.
THREE KINGS. They mean important consultations and contracts.
TWO KINGS. Professional advice or specialist medical counsel is indicated.
FOUR QUEENS. Scandal, publicity or a great debate are meant.
THREE QUEENS. They refer to a public gathering or a public discussion.
TWO QUEENS. A sincere friendship is shown.
FOUR KNIGHTS. This means police or law courts.
THREE KNIGHTS. This means the armed forces, workmen around the house, or noisy conviviality.
TWO KNIGHTS. Lawyers or doctors consult.
FOUR KNAVES. Sudden news of a serious illness of a friend comes.
THREE KNAVES. A fight or a quarrel is revealed.
TWO KNAVES. Young people cause worry.
FOUR TENS. Sudden news bringing good fortune.
THREE TENS. Hasty travel or news from overseas is shown.
TWO TENS. This means change of residence.
FOUR NINES. It means a new life or alternatively a good friend gives help.
THREE NINES. Marked success is indicated, particularly is spades are absent.
TWO NINES. They mean a gift.
FOUR EIGHTS. A parting, or a mixed success resulting in a parting, are meant.

THREE EIGHTS. They betoken marriage, or an addition to the family.

TWO EIGHTS. New surroundings, new knowledge, new studies are indicated.

FOUR SEVENS. This means the birth either of a person or of an artistic conception.

THREE SEVENS. News of illness, or illness to the client are revealed.

TWO SEVENS. A sudden surprising gift comes.

*Chapter Five*

# Methods of Reading the Tarot

As there are so many alternative meanings for each card, it is a good idea, until you have firmly committed them all to memory (which can take a very long time!) to lightly pencil the meanings on the back of each card. Reversals I consider a comparatively modern innovation, and inasmuch as there are sufficient cards of a warning or admonitory nature in the pack, there is no need to accept any reversed cards save in the Major Arcana. The reversals will modify or minimize the meanings, sometimes contradict, but no meaning is ever arbitrary. Each card is either influenced by the next card, or, if in the Major Arcana, changes by combination with others, and I would study these in the context of the whole reading. It is said that the idea of reversal and of cutting the cards with the left hand came from the same idea that the left hand is the mirror of God, in other words, the hand of the Devil, and mirrors the subconscious. (Cynics say that the Romanies used the practice of asking the female client to cut with the left hand, the ring hand, to be able to tell if she were married or single.) Pairs and three of a kind have added meanings, as well as their individual interpretations.

It is important to always remember there is no literal meaning for any card. If there are no barriers to impede the working of your sixth sense, you may find that in time, certain cards intuitively trigger off a personal message or response, a meaning quite individual and personal, which proves valid by the unfolding of your prediction.

You may also be able to evolve your own kind of memory system or mental shorthand, by associating a particular card with a symbol that has personal relevance to you or an event of personal significance which may be relevant to the card's meaning.

In order to develop a special relationship with your own Tarot pack, firstly make sure you choose a pack which appeals to your imagination, then carry it everywhere with you so that it becomes imbued with your psychic energy or special 'aura'. There are lots of packs to choose from, from the most traditional, the M1JJ, to the more esoteric Etteilla pack and the picturesque Waite pack. There are also packs put out by various societies both in England and America. Two come to mind: the American Brotherhood of Light pack, which features Egyptian symbols, in black and white, and the English Insight Institute's pack, which is based on traditional fifteenth century designs. Your pack must be protected from the vibrations of others, and it is wise to allow the minimum of handling by the client. I myself allow them to shuffle only once, and then usually at the end of the reading when I am giving them the traditional 'wish' or the 'sevens' method, used to answer a specific question or for the summing up of the entire reading or problem. You yourself should do all the laying out and most of the shuffling. Familiarize yourself with each card, by studying one card each night just before going to bed. Fix the symbols in your mind, and allow your thoughts to play with the possible enlargement of the themes of each card, or correlate certain events in your life with its meaning.

As to the actual reading of the cards, there is a lot to learn and it takes a considerable time before you become proficient and confident and even then, you will find that you are still learning.

Keeping in mind the flexibility of meanings, both knowledge and intuition must combine to master the difficult part; that of interpreting the different patterns and weaving these into a continuous, sensible narrative.

Foretelling the future carries with it a great responsibility. There is so big a margin for error, because of the nature of the cards and the fact that if we are not completely dispassionate, we may colour our reading with our own intolerances and prejudices. Never more seriously than when reading the cards, must we take into account the unique individuality of each person and his possible extreme suggestibility. We must remember the circumstances and limitations of the client, and that 'one man's meat is another man's poison'. What for us might represent a self-destructive course of action might be, for another, the means of setting him on the road to self-knowledge and fulfilment. Our words could be dangerous weapons, for sometimes they can pierce the subconscious for good or ill, so we must always be constructive, keeping in mind that these cards at times seem larger than life, and we must never exaggerate the restrictions that could be hedging the client at present or descry the possibility of future expansion commensurate with his strength and circumstances. The inner essence, the spiritual psychic and moral progression of man throughout life is the meaning of the Tarot. They reveal to us the deeper states of mind, the wasted talents, the unused strengths, the self-imposed limitations and the unvoiced desires. Until we can develop our psychic and intuitive powers to an unerring degree, which is very seldom, we must always be conscious that we are using an ability which can either be destructive or uplifting. Clairvoyance comes very close to psychotherapy, and we have to promote the cultivation of those positive attitudes which in time will eliminate the weaknesses and negative thinking that create most problems. Never dwell on the negative aspects of a reading.

There are some people who make extremely difficult subjects. You will find with these, that your intuition seems to have failed you and all that is left to do is interpret the cards as factually as you are able. Some of these will be putting a mental block up against you, as they do not believe in such a thing as the sixth sense and their opposition builds a barrier that is almost tangible. Others are so shuttered and closed in upon themselves that no chink of inner light escapes. They are usually self satisfied, rather smug people with narrow interests, their eyes fixed firmly on the ladder of material success, who feel no desire for further knowledge or self-improvement. Then there are the folk whose ability to take decisive action is severely limited but whose wish-fulfilment is so strong that it will sometimes take two or three readings to sort out the pattern of real events from the dreams or wishes. Some readings will mirror the client's state of mind at the moment so strongly that you will find you are picking up a proposed course of future events now under consideration but open to the choice of the client. Although you may advise them in their best interests, because of the presence of alternatives in the layout, you will know that they will make the wrong choice anyway. Alternatively, you may sometimes pick up, through the client's state of mind, a sense of brooding injustice, or regret for a wrong decision taken in the past, or something finished but which he will not relinquish, and you will know that this is impeding all future progress. These are the people who look backwards so often they don't see the opportunities laid at their feet. This is where clairvoyants can sometimes see further and reach a resolution to a problem more quickly than other advisers. The question of degree must be taken into account here, however, for as I have said, these cards may seem larger than life and seem to exaggerate things slightly, particularly the more mundane matters. This is the test of true experience that we learn in reading not to restrict our own views so that we misjudge the client's potential for enlargement, or give him false hopes by our exaggeration of the factors.

Until you are thoroughly conversant with the cards, do not use methods of reading which involve the use of too many cards, or you may lose direction and become confused. Use simpler smaller spreads and at first confine yourself to methods which answer one specific question. Also, it is important to impress upon the client that the Tarot cards are not too concerned with mundane selfish matters, but relate to the larger issues, so that any wish for gain must not be put in a narrow self-seeking way. For instance, when a client is asked to make a wish, he must be guided by you to concentrate on the more spiritual needs which could bring him a happier existence. If in need of money, he must not ask for a specific sum, or for money itself, but instead ask for comfort, for plenty and the means to repay all debts, financial and moral, and to live in peace.

Before you actually commence reading, try to quieten your mind and calm all mental disturbances. Start with the prayer 'God speaks through me' and think of yourself as merely a receiver set, or a channel for the images which are being transmitted to you.

When the layout or spread of cards is complete, study the entire pattern, then each individual card, then each card in relation to the next, keeping in mind that your interpretation must relate to the question asked and then to the enquirer. This is necessary because of the rather confusing various meanings for each card. It takes considerable skill and experience to link them together fluently and relate them to one another. As I have mentioned, you may find certain cards carry a basic unalterable message for you, while others alter from reading to reading.

There are many methods available to the card-reader, but I have selected the simpler spreads, mainly using only part of the entire pack. In some of these methods, more cards can be used as the reader gains proficiency and confidence, and many methods given for the use of ordinary playing cards in divination would also be suitable for the Tarot. I think it better to use quite a few different smaller layouts for the one reading than embark on a complicated pattern using all the cards, where the message may be lost through having too many things to think about at once.

When selecting the Significator card, that is, the card representing the client, use your own judgement a little in picking the type which the client most closely represents. It is usually accepted that blue eyes and brown hair with a fair skin denotes Cups or Hearts. Blonde or red hair with blue or grey eyes and the fairest of skin colouring would be represented by Pentacles or Diamonds. Clubs or Wands pertain to brown hair, hazel or brown or green eyes and a light olive skin, and Swords or Spades are represented by black hair, swarthy colouring and brown or black eyes. These rules again are not arbitrary, as there are so many different combinations in colouring, and many card-readers differ on this point. As the hair grows grey, the entire colouring becomes muted, so that older people tend to be represented by fairer cards. There are always more male court cards than female in the pack and the court cards also carry other abstract meanings apart from those which denote people, so you must be careful again not to be rigid. Knaves, as I have mentioned, can also denote a youth of either sex as well as abstract conceptions. For a man who is over thirty-five, you would choose a King; if over eighteen and under thirty-five, a Knight and under eighteen a Knave.

Before each reading, having shuffled the pack, ask the client to put the pack into three smaller packs face downwards. Pick the packs up and read the top card from each and turn over and read the bottom – before replacing the packs and proceeding with the reading, as these are signposts often giving an indication of what's to come.

## ETTEILLA'S METHOD

Shuffle the seventy-eight cards together and give them to the enquirer to cut into three piles with his left hand. Deal them, when you have put the pack together again in the same order as the enquirer cut them, from left to right, into three heaps of twenty-six cards, face downwards, one card at a time on each heap dealing from left to right. Now pick up the centre pile and set it aside. Gather the other two piles together, fifty two cards in all, shuffle them well, ask the enquirer to cut them again, and in the same manner, put the pile together and this time deal out three heaps of seventeen cards, but leave one card aside. Again, remove the middle heap and set it apart, but do not confuse it with the first heap you removed. Once more, shuffle the remaining thirty-five cards, ask the enquirer to cut them, close them up and deal three heaps of eleven cards, this time leaving two cards aside. Once more, remove the middle heap and set it apart.

Now, take the first heap of cards that was set aside, twenty-six cards in all, and lay the cards face upwards in one long row from right to left. This pile represents the soul of the enquirer, spiritual and mystic influences, the occult powers and the psychic development of the enquirer's character, and his destiny path.

Secondly, take the second heap of seventeen cards and arrange it below the first row in a similar manner. This row relates to the mental powers, intellectual capacity, hobbies, interests, affections and social nature of the enquirer.

Next, take the third pile of eleven cards and arrange them from right to left under the other two rows, so that the figure rather resembles an inverted pyramid. This third row, of course, refers to the worldly concerns, ambitions, material life, surroundings, circumstances, bodily health, carnal appetites and all appertaining to the physical domain and appetites.

When interpreting, first read each row in turn, from right to left, the opposite way from the way you have laid them out. The reading must take into consideration, apart from the ascribed meanings of each card, the proportion of each different suit in each row, and the proximity of other cards, noting particularly the reversed cards, both in context with their suit and with their individual meanings.

## ITALIAN SIMPLE METHOD

This method will yield information upon a number of points while being easy and quick.

Shuffle the entire pack and ask the enquirer to cut it three times with his left hand. Then spread the cards, face downwards like a huge fan, and ask him to choose forty eight cards and lay them one on top of the other in order. Now, still keeping this pack of forty-eight cards face downwards, deal from the top, and twelve heaps of four cards each in strict rotation. When all have been dealt, turn them over and read the piles in this order.

*Heap Number*

One: The Enquirer himself, influences and circumstances of his life

Two: Monetary affairs

Three: Family ties, relatives

Four: Close relations, offspring; their property and circumstances

Five: Love affairs, personal enjoyment and happiness

Six: Friends, fellow workers, associates

Seven: Marriage, legal affairs

Eight: Mental and physical health, accidents

Nine: The enquirer's talents, character and abilities, his future through them, his successes and rewards

Ten: The present fortunate and unfortunate influences in the enquirer's life

Eleven: Help, protection, advice, tutelage

Twelve: Unhappiness, disasters, unexpected misfortune

## THE ANCIENT CELTIC METHOD:

## THE CELTIC CROSS

Select a court card to represent the client. This card, called the Significator, is placed face upwards on the table. Give the client the pack to cut into three after you have shuffled, first asking himto concentrate on the main question he wants answered. He can either speak it aloud or remain silent. Then put the pack together again and place the first card on top of the significator. This card 'covers' him and represents the general influences around the question the client has concentrated upon. The second card is laid across the first, and although it lies on its side, is never reversed. This card 'crosses' him and shows the opposition or forces opposing the client's concerns, be they for good or evil. The third card is placed beneath the significator. This refers to what has 'gone before', meaning all that has already gone into the matter in question, or the basis of it. The fourth card is placed on the left side of the significator or 'behind him'. This shows the influences that have passed away or are just passing away. The fifth card is placed above the client's card and 'crowns' him, or represents things which may come to pass while the sixth card placed on the right of the significator is what 'lies before' him and denotes the influence that will affect him in the very near future. We have now made a cross, with the significator card covered and crossed by two cards. Now on the right hand side of the cross, in a straight line from top to bottom, place four cards in succession above one another. The seventh or bottom card represents the fears or the negative side of the client's feelings. The next, the eighth card, denotes the clients environment, the opinions and prevailing attitude of his domestic circle or friends. The third of these cards, the ninth, represents the clients own hopes and ideals concerning the matter in question and the last card, the tenth, tells the outcome of the matter.

This is the final assessment of all the other cards, plus its own meaning, and sums up the problem or gives the ultimate answer.

| | | |
|---|---|---|
| | 5<br>Crowns Him | 10<br>Final Outcome |
| | 1<br>Covering Card | 9<br>His Hopes |
| 4<br>Behind Him | Significator | 6<br>Before Him |
| | 2<br>Crossing Card | 8<br>Family Opinion |
| | 3<br>Beneath Him | 7<br>His Fears |

If the majority of the cards in this spread come from the Major Arcana then destiny will take a hand in the client's affairs and the result will be out of his hands. Should the tenth card be a court card, this also means that the result will be taken out of his hands, but more through the intervention of another person or interference, or by authority.

## THE MAJOR ARCANA QUICK SPREAD

Using the Major Arcana only, shuffle and deal three cards each in two rows thus:

| | | |
|---|---|---|
| 1 | 2 | 3 |
| 4 | 5 | 6 |

The centre cards, 2 and 5, are the decisive cards in this spread and determine the final result of the reading or the problem. The first line, cards 1, 2 and 3, presage nearer events, the bottom line those further off in time. Cards 1 and 4 denote helpful influences; cards 5 and 6 denote obstacles or the unexpected. For instance, the cards dealt might be

| 1 | 2 | 3 |
|---|---|---|
| The Hermit | The Magician | The Devil |
| 4 | 5 | 6 |
| The Empress | The Chariot | The Hanged Man |

Remembering to keep in mind that these cards are larger than life, and that there are different interpretations for this spread because of the various meanings, this is where your intuition comes into play. I would read this as follows:

The client is going to start either a new life or a new profession or work: this is shown by THE MAGICIAN. THE HERMIT appearing in the helpful influences segment means that he will proceed wisely and cautiously or would be advised to give a lot of careful thought to the way to approach things. The obstacles are denoted by THE DEVIL, which can mean an inevitable event or calamity. I would say illness, which will not be of a too serious nature, as THE HANGED MAN denotes a pause; or it could mean a sacrifice will have to be made, to ensure the triumph which THE CHARIOT brings, and the abundance, material wealth and well being, plus a return to health that THE EMPRESS presages.

## THE BOHEMIAN METHOD

First select the client's card, then shuffle, and ask the client to cut the pack into three. Note the meaning of the top card of each pack then put the pack together again and spread it out fan-wise across the table. Now, ask the client to pick twenty-one cards at random, keeping them in order of choice. Place the significator at the bottom and then deal out seven packs in the shape of a triangle as illustrated, with three cards in each pack, in a clockwise direction.

| 3<br>Friendship, Romance | 4<br>Ultimate Desire | 5<br>Unexpected help or hindrance |
|---|---|---|
| 2<br>Present desires and concerns | | 6<br>Immediate |
| 1<br>Home influence | | 7<br>Luck |

Pack No. 1. denotes home influences
Pack No. 2. denotes self, the desires and concerns of the present
Pack No. 3. denotes friendship and romance
Pack No. 4. stands for an ultimate wish or desire
Pack No. 5. denotes the unexpected, which could help or hinder No. 4.
Pack No. 6. denotes immediate influences or work in the client's life
Pack No. 7. denotes the elements of luck which affects the client's future.

## THE SEAL OF SOLOMON

First find the client's card or significator. Then shuffle the cards and ask the client to cut them into three packs. Note the meanings of the top three cards, as this can often give an indication of the general trend of the reading or the most important matter of the divination. Put the pack together again, and placing the client's card in the centre, deal out twenty-one cards in the form of a cross, placing the first at the top, the second at the bottom, the third at the left and the fourth to the right of the client's card until you have dealt out all the cards. The extra card will go into the centre pile on top of the significator and that pack is called 'To Himself'.

| | Pack One<br>'What Crowns Him' | |
|---|---|---|
| Pack Three | Pack and Significator | Pack Four |
| 'What He Faces' | 'To Himself' | 'What He Turns His Back On' |
| | Pack Two<br>'What Crosses Him' | |

The number one pack, on the top, is 'What Crowns Him', the number two pack at the bottom is 'What Crosses Him', the number three pack, to the left, is 'What Faces Him' and the number four pack at the right is 'What He Turns His Back On'.

If the enquirer is facing the number four position, 'What He Turns His Back On', it will mean that he will have the chance to rectify an error of judgement or it will mitigate the effects of a wrong decision. If however his card has its back to the number three position 'What He Faces' it means a choice is indicated and the outcome up to the client. Pack number one usually pertains to events in the far future, while number two, beneath him, usually depicts events of a transient, unimportant nature, or those concerning friends.

## THE SEVENS METHOD

This is a short method of either answering a specific question or summing up an entire reading. The reader shuffles and lays out, the client picks the cards.

Shuffle the cards and spread the entire pack face downwards on the table and ask the client to pick seven cards at random, making sure they are kept in the initial order of choice. Now, take the seven cards and lay them from right to left in this order.

7 6 5 4 3 2 1

The centre card, number four, shows client's reactions and attitudes to the matter.

Number seven shows the outcome

Number six gives the unexpected or the obstacles

Number five shows the help which may be given

Now pair off Number seven with Number one

Now pair off Number six with Number two

Now pair off Number five with Number three

Cards numbers one, two and three add clarity to the others. Number one will give some idea of the influences around the outcome; number two will show the nature of the obstacle or the unexpected and number three will specify what kind of help (or hindrance if the cards be unfortunate) will be given.

## A SIMPLE PAST, PRESENT AND FUTURE SPREAD

Shuffle the cards and deal them out in three rows from left to right, and from top to bottom, fifteen cards. The top line will indicate the future, the middle line the influence of the present and the bottom line what has already happened.

15 14 13 12 11
10 9 8 7 6
5 4 3 2 1

## THE PYRAMID

| | | | | | | | | |
|---|---|---|---|---|---|---|---|---|
| | | | 21* | | | | | 1 card |
| | | | 20 | 19 | | | | 2 cards |
| | | 18 | 17 | 16 | 15 | | | 4 cards |
| | 14* | 13 | 12 | 11 | 10 | 9 | | 6 cards |
| 8 | 7* | 6 | 5 | 4 | 3 | 2 | 1 | 8 cards |

Shuffle the pack and deal from right to left starting with number one, until you have created the pyramid, ending with card number twenty-one. Then turn over every seventh card (sometimes every fifth card is used) which will give you the general trend of the reading. The top card, number twenty-one, will show the most important influences now dominating the client, and must be considered in relation to all the other cards. The bottom line often pertains to the past of the client.

After shuffling and cutting the cards, put the pack together and deal out the first seven cards in an anti-clockwise direction as illustrated.

Card Number One – Past influences
Card Number Two – Present circumstances
Card Number Three – The general future
Card Number Four – The best policy to follow
Card Number Five – the attitude of others around
Card Number Six – Obstacles in the way of the solution to the question
Card Number Seven – The final outcome

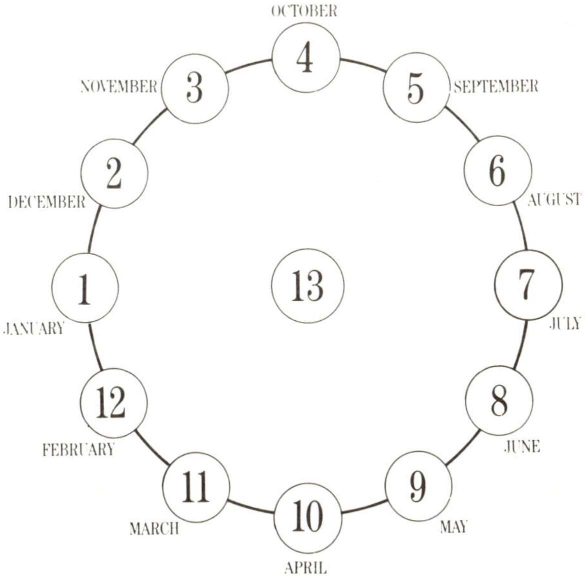


**THE YEAR AHEAD**

This circular spread gives a forecast of the year ahead beginning from the date of the reading, and is the only method in which both the client and the reader shuffle.

Shuffle the cards. Ask the client to shuffle the pack and then return it to you. From the top of the pack deal out twelve cards in a circle clockwise, face upwards, then place the thirteenth card in the middle commencing from the left as illustrated. The last card, number thirteen, should be read first, as it is the ruling card, giving the tone of the whole year. Now the cards are read in sequence but this time in an anti-clockwise direction. As the cards are laid down, some of them may be placed in a reversed position – but they are read as being upright. Each card denotes a month in the coming year.

## SOME READINGS I HAVE GIVEN

### THE BOHEMIAN METHOD

The client cut the pack into three and the first three cards turned up were the THREE OF HEARTS, THE FOUR OF STAVES and THE FIVE OF SWORDS. This meant that the client would have to accept the inevitable, possibly having to swallow his pride before he cleared the decks for a new life which would begin for him.

*Pack Number One: The Six of Spades, The King of Wands and The Four of Pentacles*
There will be success after anxiety; a big obstacle will be removed. A man may leave his home and thus solve a long standing problem. There will be help from a powerful man.

*Pack Number Two: The Lovers, Temperance and The Knight of Swords*
If the client wishes to foster a romance he must make concessions, as he will have a rival for the affections of someone, and there will be a choice to make, possibly requiring more adaptability than the client possesses.

*Pack Number Three: The Two of Staves, The Nine of Swords and The Page of Wands*
A disillusionment or disappointment, or deep sadness will be brought by news. It could possibly be the end of an ambition, but the help of a powerful man brings benefits from another direction. Strength of will and spiritual depth are also indicated and the client will succeed in another direction entirely.

*Pack Number Four: The Knight of Pentacles, The Star and The Five of Wands*
This person is highly intuitive himself and possesses great gifts and a desire for self improvement and achievement.

4
Ultimate Desire

3
Friendship,
Romance

5
Unexpected help or
hindrance

2
Present desires and
concerns

6
Immediate

1
Home
influence

7
Luck

THE STAR means that he will widen all horizons and will be given a lot of help in achieving his aims. It will be hard and he will have to battle, there will be many tests and a few defeats. He will achieve much, although there will be many rivals in his chosen field of work and fluctuations in his fortune. He will change his residence, and possibly go overseas or emigrate. He can expect success.

*Pack Number Five: The Seven of Pentacles, The Two of Swords and The Three of Wands*
This pack means that the client's efforts will be rewarded. There will be new opportunities opening up and new skills to be developed after a frustrating period of delay and indecision. He will gain equilibrium in his affairs, and must make every effort to push his interests, as the future promises wonderful success in employment, where original ideas, creative talent and inspirational collective activities all will play a part in the realization of an ambition.

*Pack Number Six: The Three of Cups, The Ten of Staves and The Page of Cups*
The immediate future will bring rejoicing, from a victory, news or a message. A burden will soon be dropped or the client will reach a goal. A problem will soon be solved, although the client will insist on doing things the hard way.

*Pack Number Seven: The King of Pentacles, The Ace of Pentacles and The Five of Pentacles*

Enforced restriction, or unemployment, will lead to greater opportunities, along with severe material adversity, but the client will gain help from a practical, wise and loyal man. He has the stoicism and strength to endure, and will build a secure foundation. He longs for material comfort, which will be his after struggles.

This client interested me very much, as he is a very young man, who even at the age of twenty-two is a leader of a spiritualist church, and shows great psychic power. He is conscious of his lack of formal education and is eager to learn. He would like to study at night school so that he can obtain the requisite qualifications to be able to practise some form of social work, and at the time of the reading had applied for a position with a welfare organization that offered training. He also has a romantic interest, which at the time did not seem satisfactory. At the house where he was living, he had a problem with a neurotic neighbour. He faces a victory and then a defeat out of which comes a wonderful chance for progress through the help of a powerful man, and has the strength to endure the disappointment. His domestic problem will be solved, but his love life did not look so hopeful, as he tends to be rather intolerant of the weaknesses of others at times, and is a little too serious for his own good.

N.B. He later obtained a post as prison officer and later became a well known spiritualist medium – and now has a church of his own.

## THE PYRAMID METHOD

*Using Every Fifth Card as a Signpost*

When the pack was cut into three, the cards uppermost were:

THE MAGICIAN THE WORLD THE KNIGHT OF CUPS

The top card, number twenty-one, plus the three cards turned up when the pack was cut, give the tone of the reading, and

<table>
<tr><td></td><td></td><td></td><td colspan="2">21<br>Justice</td><td></td><td></td><td></td></tr>
<tr><td></td><td></td><td></td><td>20<br>The Ten of<br>Swords</td><td>19<br>The King of<br>Pentacles</td><td></td><td></td><td></td></tr>
<tr><td></td><td></td><td>18<br>The<br>World</td><td>17<br>The Ten<br>of Wands</td><td>16<br>The Three<br>of Swords</td><td>15<br>The Page<br>of Cups</td><td></td><td></td></tr>
<tr><td></td><td>14<br>The Ace<br>of Cups</td><td>13<br>The Ten<br>of Cups</td><td>12<br>The Nine<br>of Wands</td><td>11<br>The Queen<br>of Swords</td><td>10<br>The High<br>Priestess</td><td>9<br>The Six<br>of Wands</td><td></td></tr>
<tr><td>8<br>The Four<br>of Swords</td><td>7<br>The<br>Moon</td><td>6<br>The Four<br>of Cups</td><td>5<br>The Ten of<br>Pentacles</td><td>4<br>The Queen<br>of Wands</td><td>3<br>The<br>Star</td><td>2<br>The Five of<br>Pentacles</td><td>1<br>The Ace of<br>Pentacles</td></tr>
</table>

every fifth card acts as a signpost. The enquirer was female, and young, and evidently there was a new life, possibly full attainment, and/or travel through or with a fairish young man. The card number twenty-one could pertain to actual law suits, or could determine the result of a moral question, but in this case, as it turned out, I was correct in thinking the young man in question was a lawyer.

The bottom line, numbers one to eight, always seem to denote the immediate past and I told the young lady that she had been out of work but had recently secured a new position, that she or her mother had received some money from a will, but that plans for the purchase of a house had been delayed or frustrated. She agreed that this was so. I then told her that she might have a little operation and period of convalescent, or had already had this. She told me she had to go into hospital for a minor matter the following week.

The next line was the most interesting, as it dealt with the young man who turned up in those first three cards. I said I thought there could be a lot of happiness ahead for them both, but a woman stood between her and her wish as the young man, although he would achieve triumph in the sphere of his work, and evidently had more study or examinations to do, was being hindered in some way by a woman. I then asked whether he was a widower, and she said yes, and he would not remarry, mainly because his wife had prevented him from completing his law degree while alive, through envy and possessiveness.

I then read the third line and said that in my opinion, just when things looked as if they might crystallize, the young man's problems would be solved by news of an offer from overseas, and I had the feeling that it was a scholarship or something entailing further study. This would mean disappointment and delay for her: possibly she would wait for him to return. I sincerely hoped so, but felt that the young man was deliberate and cautious to an extreme, and balanced all factors in his mind rather too dispassionately. The presence of THE TEN OF SPADES also means the lowest point in a community's fortune. But in this case I felt it brought pain and tears and the end of a dream that was based on too much deliberation or fear of committal, and thought my client would grow tired of waiting.

Every fifth card – THE TEN OF PENTACLES, THE HIGH PRIESTESS, THE PAGE OF CUPS and THE TEN OF SWORDS – could be read as the dream of setting up a home and starting a married life, which would be shattered through news to do with education.

There are at least four other ways one could interpret these cards and each one could be correct, but refer to something else, or the same matter in a different way. This was the message that I received, and as it happened, it was substantially correct.

Although, as it was a recent reading, I have not as yet heard the latest developments, except that the young man in question had applied for an overseas grant to study at a university in America and at the time of reading had not told his lady friend, but on hearing about the reading, informed her it was practically 'cut and dried'.

## THE PAST, PRESENT AND FUTURE SPREAD

In the past there has been adversity or suffering, and possibly a change has been made, and there has been difficulty in launching a new project. There could also have been past influences affecting the client or parental opposition to a love affair, or an emotional choice which caused suffering. The client has had to carefully control matters and finances to achieve a difficult balance.

The present shows that the struggles were not in vain, and security in the material sense is now evident through successful business transactions. It is a time to be up and doing, a time of great possibilities. If referring to a love affair, there will be a happy and wealthy marriage and the client will find his judgement and his character or that of his loved one, vindicated.

The future promises stability, a loving union and/or perhaps a business partnership or the signing of either marriage or business contracts. The main obstacles to progress will have been removed and the client will possibly move to more harmonious surroundings, and leave behind his former unhappiness.

You will note that I have allowed for the fact that there could be at least two interpretations, such as marriage and business contracts. Often both can apply, but in this case I intuitively felt it pertained to a difficult and stormy romance with parental or other opposition, and the client confirmed this. You might read this differently again. This is the point where the intuition takes over.

The Past, Present and Future Spread

| 1 | 2 | 3 | 4 | 5 |
|---|---|---|---|---|
| | | FUTURE | | |
| Six of Swords | Kings of Pentacles | Ace of Wands | Two of Cups | Eight of Swords |
| | | PRESENT | | |
| THE EMPRESS | Queens of Wands | Ten of Pentacles | Seven of Wands | JUSTICE |
| | | PAST | | |
| Ace of Swords | Six of Cups | THE LOVERS | TEMPERANCE | Two of Pentacles |

## GLOSSARY OF TERMS

ADEPT A person who has gained proficiency in any art or science. When used in the occult sense, it means a person who has successfully passed through the initiatory stages and could now be considered a master of one or more of the branches of occult science.

ALCHEMY The science of changing or transmuting things: this means changing the essential nature of something to produce something finer. Alchemy deals with two levels, the physical as where the ancient alchemists tried to turn base metals into gold, or to create elixirs to restore lost youth, and the philosophical level of purifying and transforming the baser passions into the spiritual.

ARCANE Another term for the occult.

ARCANUM This was the name of an elixir used by ancient occultists to stimulate the powers of prophecy.

ASTARTE The most important of all the Phoenician goddesses. She was the Semitic fertility goddess, the counterpart of Aphrodite and as she was considered also to rule the moon, love and beauty, could also be considered the Semitic Diana.

ATLANTIS That fabled lost continent has been the subject of conjecture since Plato's time, when he claimed that had it not been for a spirited counter-offensive by the Greeks, the Atlanteans would have overrun Europe. The continent, supposedly situated in the Atlantic, was thought to have been destroyed by either a series of eruptions or a tidal wave. There is an occult belief that Lemuria or Mu exists beneath the waves of the South Pacific and is a sister continent of Atlantis. The inhabitants are thought to have been kin to the Mayas and the Incas and, because of their knowledge which was too advanced for their time, most were said to have perished in a gigantic flood when Lemuria sank beneath the sea, leaving the South Pacific islands as the only visible evidence of their existence.

AUGUR A priest in ancient Rome who studies the flight and migratory habits of birds and predicted the course of events from such study.

CADUCEUS A cosmic magical and astronomical symbol, depending upon its application. The wand of Hermes, or Mercury, it originally featured a triple-headed serpent with the property of inducing sleep, but modern medicine, in adopting it as a symbol, uses only two serpents, one black and one white, to signify disease and cure and has the two wings of Mercury on top.

CHARMS AND TALISMANS These are magical notes on formulae which can be drawn, written, recited or sung over an object in order to imbue it with certain magical properties and powers, believed to effect a desired result or state of being. These objects could be of any material substance, but the most common were talismans, amulets and lucky stones. The amulets or bracelets were often worn to ward off the Evil Eye or evil spirits and give protection, while the talismans were sometimes worn, either as inscribed parchment or cloth, as a pendant hanging from a chain, to endow the wearer with certain powers, strengths or abilities.

COSMIC The definition of cosmic in the Rosicrucian manual is 'The

Divine Infinite Intelligence or the Supreme Being Permeating Everything, the Creative Forces of God'.

COSMIC CONSCIOUSNESS That super-awareness, possessed by very few, of the life-pattern of the universe and the ultimate goal of the ever-developing spirit.

COSMIC LEMNISCATE A figure shaped like an eight lying on its side which the ancient Egyptians believed represented the eternal cosmic forces, for it had neither end nor beginning.

CULT A series of rituals and practices built into a corporate body of belief which is devoted to the worship of one particular divine concept or divine being.

DEMI-URGE The force which created all matter, in the Gnostic creed. The inferior, evil, the material element, as opposed to the divine, superior creator of the spirit.

DIANA The Roman goddess of the moon and the hunt, and the ruler of wild animals. Often equated with the Greek goddess Artemis.

DRUIDS A magical people who practised their rites in a wide domain covering France, England and Ireland, and were very powerful among the Celtic races before the advent of Christianity. They were skilled in all kinds of magic, astrology and alchemy.

EARTH MOTHER Many of the most powerful goddesses in the pantheons of the polytheistic religions were so styled because of their supposed power over the forces of nature.

ESOTERIC Secret traditions: facts usually not accessible to the uninitiated, usually pertaining to secret doctrine, secret rites and secret philosophy. When made public the facts become exoteric.

ENLIGHTENMENT The knowledge of God achieved through spiritual development.

THE THREE FATES Clotho the spinner, Lachesis the disposer and Atropos, the unchangeable, who snips the thread of life.

FEMININE PRINCIPLE The feminine principle, or feminine force, in occult lore represents one part of the cosmic pattern – the passive, negative, receptive and regenerative aspects which are always considered feminine in quality. The female goddesses in the pantheons usually stood for the material and physical forces of nature, nourishment and intuitive wisdom.

GOAT OF MENDES Usually depicted with four horns, this figure derives from an Egyptian deity, a form of Pan. Later it was associated with black magic and as the 'bachelor', was the goat-like body which the Devil was supposed to assume on the witches' sabbath when he came down to earth and had intercourse with the witches. He was then known as the Sabbatic Goat. Also, this figure became known as a Baphomet, which was the word for an idol of any kind, but which possibly derived from statues fashioned for the cults who worshipped Saturn, Mithras or Dionysus. Most of these portrayed Saturn in many guises, one of which was a horned figure with a beard.

GNOSTICISM Derived from the Greek word for knowledge, it was a creed composed of many elements from the philosophies and beliefs of Babylon, India, Persia and Egypt, and embodies as well some of the elements of the Hebrew Qabbala and the Christian religion. The Gnostic priests practised astrology, numerology and the arts of magic, and some sects appear to have celebrated the Greek mysteries in a slightly debased form. They flourished in the Roman Empire at the time of Christ, their headquarters being Alexandria.

GRIMOIRE A general expression used to cover those books containing information, spells, incantations and alchemical experiments often used in early centuries against the Qabbala and later written to promote Devil worship, and giving instructions for Devil worship.

GYPSIES A contraction of the word Egyptian, but not pertaining to Egypt but rather to Palestine or 'Little Egypt' from where it was believed the wandering tribes of people came. They were gifted with clairvoyance as well as the ability to cast spells, possessed the Evil Eye, and were versed in all kinds of magic.

HECATE Queen of the night, the Dark Moon who brought madness to those who defied her and who guarded the gates of Hades. She commanded all the magical powers of nature, and ruled sorcery and magic.

HERMES TRISMEGISTOS Hermes, messenger of the gods, also identified with the ibis-headed Egyptian god Thoth, inventor of the magical arts and of the art of writing, god of wisdom and patron of the arts. Said to have conceived the *Book of Thoth* or *Book of the Dead*, a collection of magical writings found on papyri, as well as in tombs and on monuments. These were neo-Platonic astrological and alchemical works.

HIEROPHANT A teacher, an adept who has attained the status and experience requisite for the imparting of sacred esoteric knowledge to others.

ISIS Wife of Osiris, she was the greatest of all ancient Egyptian goddesses and had many facets. Some of her titles included 'she who is the beginning', 'she who is without end', 'mistress of magic', 'speaker of the spells', 'the only true bestower of Life'. Her influence was very wide, particularly around the Mediterranean and the Egyptian mysteries commemorating the death and resurrection of Osiris, which still exist in some forms to this day.

JANUS Roman two-headed god of doorways, and later god of beginnings.

JUNO Wife of Jupiter, queen of the Roman gods, ruler of marriage and chastity.

JUPITER King of the Roman gods, identified with the Zeus of the Greeks and with Ammon of Egypt.

KABALA or QABBALA A leading theosophical system of the Hebrews, evolved during the Middle Ages, of mystical spells, rituals and incantations, which was outlawed by the orthodox religion. It was based on an occult interpretation of the Bible and was handed down in an esoteric tradition to the students of the occult.

KEY OF SOLOMON A magical Grimoire or collection of writings said to have been written by King Solomon, but believed to have been written in either the fourteenth or fifteenth centuries.

KISMET The Arabic word for fate. Moslems believe that a man's life is fated and the course is inevitable.

LAUREL A tree whose leaf has long been considered magical. It symbolized divinity and favour of the gods. Sacred to Venus, it was considered to be a protection against evil spirits. It also denoted royalty, victory and power, and ancient Romans believed that to dream of a laurel wreath presaged national fame and high honours.

LIGHTNING Forked lightning was considered to be a symbol of sacred power.

MALE PRINCIPLE The masculine force: in occult lore, the active, positive aspect of the cosmic law and pattern.

MANDALA A psychic symbol denoting wholeness. Usually of a circular shape, with a symbol of the self in the centre and other symbols at each corner.

MITHRAISM This cult, open only to the masculine sex, was very popular in the Roman Empire, particularly with the army, although it originated in Persia. The god hero Mithras gave up his life on earth to service of mankind and later, upon his ascension to heaven, he continued to exert his influence among his followers in their struggle against evil. The Mithraists practised elaborate initiation ceremonies which were graded in seven stages, corresponding to their seven grades of heaven which culminated in the dwelling of the Ineffable.

THE MUSES The nine daughters of Zeus and Mnemosyne. Each muse ruled over an art or science and they gave divine inspiration to the poet, painter and author.

THE MYSTERIES In these ancient rites, the priests, initiate and neophytes acted in allegorical tableaux that featured the deities, the secret significance of which was explained to the initiates upon their gaining their 'crown', or after passing the Dionysian mystery cult.

THE DIONYSIAN MYSTERY CULT This cult originated in Phrygia and began as an orgiastic celebration, with the sacrifice of animals and the drinking of blood. Later these rites took on a deeper, more spiritual significance, and were called the Orphic mysteries. They incorporated belief in reincarnation.

THE ELEUSIAN MYSTERIES This was the oldest of the mystery cults which originated nine hundred years before Christ in Eleusis. It was centred around the 'earth mother' Demeter and her daughter Persephone, the regenerating principle, and was agrarian in nature.

NEOPHYTE A new convert, a novice.

OSIRIS The husband of Isis, the father of Horus, worshiped as the maker of heaven and earth.

PAN The all-encompassing: associated with Priapus and, later, the Maypole, he was a cloven-hoofed, horned and primitive prototype of the 'all father'. Pan was the god of hunting and of forests, and patron of shepherds, who embodied the primitive forces of nature.

PERSEPHONE Daughter of Demeter, the 'earth mother' and wife of Hades, the king of hell, who was returned to her mother for eight months in every year.

PHRYGIAN CAP Sacred to the Rosicrucians, always red in colour, it is said to be phallic in origin, deriving from circumcision. Possibly derives from an ancient representation of Hermes, who was depicted wearing a herdsman's cap of a similar shape. The magician is sometimes shown wearing a cap like this.

ROSE Sacred to Venus and used in love potions this flower has been regarded by many cultures as sacred and a symbol of life, love and beauty. The Greeks regarded it as a sign of silence, and it was used as a decoration in the robes of the initiate in the crowning ceremony in the mysteries.

SHAMAN Shamanism is the primitive belief in discarnate intelligence or in spirits whose priests or medicine men practised rites which they believed gave them the power over or the control of such spirits so that they could exorcise them or command them to appear. It is used now in a general sense to describe any application of methods of magic in order to communicate with or control unseen forces considered to be supernatural or superhuman.

SISTRUM The sacred rattle of Isis, always denoting joy and merriment.

TITANS In Greek mythology, a race of giants who attacked and fought the gods for supremacy.

UNICORN The beautiful mythical creature famed for its magical ability, associated with the moon and the female element. It was small and white, looked rather like a beautiful horse and had one curled horn in the middle of its forehead. It could only be lured and captured by a virgin, who would sit in a wood where it would trustfully approach her and put its head in her lap.

*Chapter Six*

# The Gambling Cards

I have left until this chapter a few other interesting views concerning the origin of the Tarot, because I think it is time we delved into the fascination of gambling and deal briefly with cards used for that purpose. Although they too, can be used for divination – as you will learn later – craftsmen and artists of every nation, for thousands of years, have produced little masterpieces in the interests of gambling, for the lure of luck, the element of risk attendant upon the flicking of a die or the turn of a card has been a universal attraction since time immemorial.

It is believed that card playing derives from the ancient practice of primitive tribes of throwing arrows into a hallowed or magical circle for the purpose of divination. In Korea, today, there exists a game called *Nyout* which derives from this ancient practice, common to other primitive peoples such as the American Indian, and the Korean cards, which are very long and thin still bear an arrow stencilled on their backs.

Chess had its origin in a game played before the days of Troy by shepherds of western Asia. The game featured the use of pebbles in a divided square, with a sheepfold in the centre. From this game came both the later roman game of draughts and a game known as *Petteia*, which gradually assumed a more military character and became the forerunner of our modern chess.

Another ancient game, that of *Mora*, still played today and known to have been played in the time of Moses in ancient Egypt, may also have derived form *Petteia*; draught boards and gaming-boards were depicted on murals found in the tombs of the pharaohs, and one such tomb, that of Tutankhamen, in recent times, yielded up a beautiful example of a gaming-board of inlaid ivory and gold.

The game was possibly taken to China by a tribe of wandering Hindus, for it had long been known in Arabia, Persia and India in its original form. They gave it a unique Chinese character which it retains to this day, for they settled across the river from the fierce marauding Tartars, and the Chinese chessboard still shows a space in the middle of the board representing this river or barrier, while the chess pieces mirror the warlike character of the protagonists.

Papus noticed a similarity between the 'coat' or court cards, so named for their elaborate robes, and some of the chess pieces, such as the kings and queens, the tower, the bishop and the knave. He also commented upon the fact that the earlier boards the Crusaders brought back with them had numbered squares which early philosophers had used to solve problems of logic. He thought that if the numbers were separated and made into a die and the pictured trumps placed around a wheel, we should then have the game of *Goose* with which Ulysses practised cheating beneath the walls of Troy. It may well have been *Petteia* Ulysses played, but the game of *Goose* was of much later origin.

B'Oiteau D'Ambley's theory that the Tarot had an oriental origin, having been brought by the Romans to Europe via India, is true in one particular. So may be the observation by Papus, of the similarity of the Tarot with the chess pieces denoting a common origin, for the Tarot is thought to have been based on an amalgamation of Chinese chess pieces and gambling cards. These are the earliest known cards in existence, and date back to the eleventh century. The cards were apparently based on the design of paper money which had been introduced into China in the T'ang dynasty, some time between 600 AD and the end of the tenth century. Marco Polo remarked upon this paper money, which was later copied by Venetian and Italian traders who brought it back to Europe. Apparently real money was used sometimes in China in these games. Cards in China were also interchangeable with dominoes, the latter being used for fortune telling and decorated with different flowers, animals and folk heroes. Possibility the cards and dominoes were brought to Europe, and the card makers adapted and Europeanised the Chinese signs and symbols without knowing their significance, resulting in the traditional suit signs and our court cards.

There has also been a vague suggestion that the Tarot could have an Indian origin. This was based on the Romany theory and the fact that there could be a slight analogy between the Cups relating to priests or Brahmins, the Swords to the warrior, the Coins to the merchants, and the Batons to the serfs or peasants. The Major Arcana, it was observed, had certain similarities with the divine concepts of Buddha. However, these delineations of Cups, Wands, Deniers and Swords, could just as well apply to the different strata of medieval Italy, or as we have seen to the Grail Hallows, and the symbology of the Tarot could be considered universal. There is now view that Indian playing cards actually derived from the European cards, and that their circular shape may have come from their original interchangeability with chess pieces, as in China. The Indian cards have eight or ten suits, and their symbology, which is mainly religious, derives from the ten reincarnations of Vishnu.

Samuel Singer, in the nineteenth century, stated that *Trappolo* was the earliest game played in Europe and was introduced by the Arabs, by way of Italy. Covelluzo, however, writing in the fifteenth century, stated that the Saracens introduced the game *Naib* into Italy in 1379 when the rival Popes, Clement VII and Urban VI, engaged mercenaries from Arabia to fight in their private armies. However, Arabs had been living in Spain as early as the eighth century, had also been in Italy before 1379 and had penetrated before that time as far as Arles in France and into Sicily. This theory comes up against those experts who point out that, if cards did originate in Arabia, it is odd that there is no mention of them in *The Arabian Nights*. Of course it is possible that cards were banned, but it is strange that such a forbidden and alluring pastime would not somewhere form the basis of a tale of delight and punishment. In any case, the Saracens' Muslim religion forbade both gambling and drawing human figures, so it is unlikely that the Tarot originated with them.

Singer says that the Semitic word for card play is *naipes*, the derivation of our 'Jack O'Napes', and it is a fact that the ancient game of *Roccambo*, played in Spain, used the Tarot suits; but the word naipes could have come from the Flemish word *knaep*, for paper, for there was much trade between Flanders and Spain, and as card-making became an industry many countries exported cards.

Playing cards, as we have seen, were the subject of many decrees; some protests against gambling, such as the decrees issued in Paris prohibiting play on working days, some like that of Henry VII of England, whose own daughter Margaret apparently shared the gambling fever with her father's subjects. He forbade servitors and apprentices to gamble at any time save during the Christmas holiday period – thus protecting the card-making industry.

Although the Tarot remained the everyday cards, for the stencilled packs, although cheap and flimsy, were well within the reach of the working classes, famous artists and goldsmiths were commissioned to design more elaborate packs for rich private patrons, as we have seen with the Visconti pack, and this practice continued up to the days of the French Revolution. Indeed, there were playing cards of silver at the court of Louis XV of France. After the stencil, came the wood block printing thought to have arrived in Germany with the coming of traders who had travelled to Russia from China by way of Arabia. The very first wood engravings may well have been playing cards, for the earliest known examples in existence are the 'Little Saints', illustrations of saints and ecclesiastical subjects printed in the monasteries, but which could have been adapted from the dimensions and techniques used by the earliest German card-makers. This new process made cards cheaper, more durable and more easily available to the public.

The decree by Edward IV forbidding the import of foreign cards into England shows the extent of their popularity and the rapidity of the growth of the card-making industry. Although most countries manufactured cards, France remained the greatest exporter. Bordeaux, for instance, made cards expressly for the Spanish market, called *Hombre* packs, and other centres in France exported cards to England, Holland, Bavaria, Germany and South America, all fashioned to suit the tastes and attitudes of each country.

The English cards of the Tudor period, sometimes made in France, and called 'decks' of cards or sometimes 'paires', mirrored the fashions at court. In Henry VII's time they showed the ladies with the lappets over their ears, and the knaves with their flat caps and red, yellow and green stockings, while later cards, in Elizabeth's reign, depicted the Queens with the crowns perched perilously on the back of their heads.

A century before the first wood engravings a French knight, Etienne Vignoles, created a new pack and a new game called Piquet. This game was based on the rules of chivalry, and used only thirty-eight cards, dropping all the threes, fours and fives, the Page and the trumps of the Tarot. The suit signs were changed to Cups for the Church, Carreaux or arrowheads for the archers or vassals, Trefles or clover for the farmer and piques or the point of the lance for the knights. The court cards were often named for famous knights such as Lancelot or kings such as Alexander. From these innovations come our modern suit emblems of cups, diamonds, clubs and spades. Some authorities think the suit of Carreaux, our diamonds, symoblised the tiles on the floors of the merchants' exchanges and represented the medieval guilds, rather than the archers and their arrowheads. Our suit of spades, the 'Piques' of Piquet, are named for the Spanish *espadas* or Swords, and our diamonds may have been influenced more by the Spanish money suit than by the Carreaux in Piquet.

So there were two kinds of packs used concurrently, the Tarot and the Piquet pack, and each, as the industry grew, became more elaborate and the designs and decorations more diversified. With the advent of printing, the working man also could afford to pick and choose from patience packs, fortune-telling packs, Piquet packs, and even Tarots had many kinds of different trumps, even though the older traditional Tarot still remained a firm favourite, particularly in the southern districts of France.

Educational card games were invented, the earliest being the work of a teaching Franciscan monk, Thomas Murner, in Switzerland at the beginning of the sixteenth century, as an aid to teaching philosophy. One famous pack was devised by Cardinal Mazarin for young King Louis XIV, and executed by a member of the French Academy, and included such subjects as geography, history, kings and queens of France, Greek mythology and a charming set illustrated with some of Aesop's fables. The earliest spiritual card game was invented by a Carmelite Father, Joseph of Antwerp in 1666, and was illustrated with incidents from biblical tales and texts. Later, with the Pope's approval, a Cloister series was published, made expressly for ecclesiastical and monastic orders on much the same lines. Early children's games ranged from alphabetical sets to games teaching military science. There were also books published like *Le Passetemps de la Fortune* in 1634, giving instructions for foretelling with dice, interpretations of dreams and methods of divination with playing cards.

Famous artists and goldsmiths were commissioned in every European capital to produce appealing packs of cards as gambling became the pastime of the wealthy. In Britain, a gaming master was added to the list of tutors necessary to educate well born young ladies and gentlemen in the social graces, books were printed giving rules and procedures of gaming, and the first history of playing cards was published in 1704.

French and German court cards featured reigning monarchs as well as court dandies. English cards depicted the Gunpowder Plot, the Horrid Popish Plot, the Spanish Armada, John Gay's *Beggars' Opera*, and even commemorated the South Sea Bubble scandal; while some Dutch packs also satirized the Bubble Disaster and political subjects. Viennese cards included a set of Tarots with the trumps depicting famous stage personalities. Anything and everything became the subject of the trumps, from animal Tarots to famous ballerinas and different dances and operettas, and later cards even illustrated characters from the novels of Sir Walter Scott.

However, when Napoleon came to power, he relegated all the court cards to waste paper baskets and commissioned such famous neo-classicists as the artist and sculptor David to design new packs of cards depicting worthy but rather dull subjects such as revolutionary heroes, gods and goddesses of ancient Greece and Rome (with Napoleon himself as Caesar!). There was naturally a later series featuring the French front line regiments and all the great French victories against the English. Not surprisingly, a later French set commemorated Wellington's victories against the French. But this new fashion was not popular, and after Napoleon's final defeat, the card-makers, many of whom had gone out of business, resumed making their fanciful cards and the only innovation which did not lose its appeal was the fortune-telling pack of Marie le Normand, and of course the many books published during the Napoleonic period on the popular methods of divination. There had been a pack of divinatory cards issued to commemorate Napoleon's return, which soon went out of existence.

There were Tarot cards made in England reflecting the craze for chinoiserie that swept through the Regency period while Holland produced beautiful patience packs with oriental subjects and heraldic cards came from every country. The Joker was introduced in America in the middle of the nineteenth century for the new game of euchre and the later American packs featured subjects such as cartoon comic characters, army and navy series and even a pack depicting bicycles of every kind. One featured the methods of cooking meat and other dishes, and was in fact an early cookery book. As late as 1915, there was a satirical pack of cards made in Australia with a wartime patriotic flavour, with caricatures of the reigning British monarch and national leaders as the trumps. In spite of all the interesting subjects, beautiful designs, witty verses and clever presentations, these beautifully designed cards never succeeded in equalling the powerful appeal of the original fourteenth century. Tarots, which remain today, after six hundred years, mysterious and fascinating.

*Chapter Seven*

# Cartomancy

## THE PICTURES ON THE CARDS

*The Court Cards*

These have nothing of human emotion or sympathy in their expression but seem detached yet strangely understanding.

The suits of Diamonds and Hearts are red, while Clubs and Spades are black.

The Queen of Hearts carries her flowers on the right, the other three Queens carry theirs on the left. The male Court Cards all bear their rods or swords on the left side. The King of Diamonds, the Jack of Hearts and the Jack of Spades are shown with one eye only. The emblems commonly used on the cards or suggested in various patterns are the cross, the whirling circle, the Sunflower, the rectangle, the triangle, the circle and the Fleur de Lis.

The King of Hearts is depicted with two pairs of hands. The raised pair, holding an emblem of power denotes strength and authority, the lowered pair depict the power of peace of love.

The King of Diamonds carries a Battle-Axe. The left hand, carrying the weapon is hidden, while the right points to the suit symbol, which signifies precious metal or mineral wealth such as diamonds.

The King of Clubs wears a sunflower as his belt buckle and his sword has a wavy edge. His is the only card bearing a symbol of the girdled universe, which is said to represent conquest of the world through intellect, power and action.

The King of Spades is sometimes depicted as wearing the symbol of Trinity on his breast-plate and he and his Queen face away from their suit symbol, as if facing the light.

The Queen of Hearts is the only Queen who is not facing a flower, or sometimes a candle – the symbol of hope, intuition and mental inspiration, while the Queen of Diamonds wears a massive jewelled neckband, possibly indicating the yoke of wealth. In some packs, the Queen of Clubs carries a swastika – one of the oldest good luck emblems – on her belt linked by wheels.

The Jack of Hearts holds a yellow feather or leaf, suggesting fickleness, and, unaware of the battle-axe at his back seems to be portraying a light hearted attitude to life.

The Jack of Diamonds has only his fingers showing on the rod behind him and is often portrayed wearing 3 diamonds on his breastplate – suggesting wealth and stealth.

The Jack of Clubs faces a pointed stave – and has a leaf suspended from his crown – sometimes he is depicted as wearing a peculiar kind of cross on his breastplate. The leaf and stave could denote agricultural toil and wealth.

The Jack of Spades faces an hour glass as if seeing into time itself – possibly denoting a sense of karmic destiny.

## THE SIGNIFICANCE OF THE SUITS

*Hearts*

Hearts represent joy – sensitivity – spiritual interests, love and affection. The ancient suit was that of Cups, and taken from that standpoint it could represent the home – the bank the purse – supply – partnership – realisation – assets and resources. This is the strongest suit emotionally.

*Diamonds*

Diamonds are nearly always connected with monetary affairs, influence and affluence. They refer to material struggle and denote ideas coupled with production. They refer to the merchant, the professional and the labourer. The ancient symbology of Coins represented money or charity – political eminence, family dynasties, law-suits and profit, opportunity. Such things as jewellery, clothes, manufacturing and building construction, all come under the influence of Diamonds. This is the strongest suit materially.

*Clubs*

This suit was known in ancient times as Wands or Sceptres. This is artistically the strongest suit and it rules such things as talent, endeavour optimism, justice, sagacity, order and development and solid material success. Clubs show the power of the Sitter and what he could make of his own destiny. They indicate, as opposed to the more material Diamonds, serenity of character, an optimistic, philosophical outlook, inner security and love of craft. The ancients considered this suit to be the bulwark between mental activity and material desire, and the meanings are underlaid by the desire for spiritual wisdom.

*Spades*

Although traditionally the Spades, which derived from swords, represent the physical sense by inversion, they also stand for spiritual strength and knowledge – so are the strongest spiritual suit. Beneath their surface meaning they have a deeper inner significance. Although they stand for the Government, police and medical as well as legal concerns, they also denote self awareness, self discipline, self conquest, through trial, loss and suffering.

Some point to remember when Reading:

Should Diamonds outnumber Hearts in a lay-out the Sitter must guard over greed and domination of others.

Should Diamonds and Spades be closely connected the Sitter will triumph over seemingly insurmountable difficulties.

Should Hearts predominate the Sitter is a dreamer who must learn to control the emotions. Clubs always show movement in an upward direction – particularly the cards from ace to seven which denote speed and efficiency.

Should Clubs predominate the Sitter's life will be balanced and blessed as long as he or she doesn't become a 'workaholic'.

Should Spades predominate the Sitter is learning his or her lessons now – some would say in his or her last and final life.

## SIGNIFICANCE OF EACH SUIT CARD FOR THE PURPOSE OF CARD-READING

*Suit of Hearts*
*Ace.* The House or Home. Pertaining to love, warmth and passion, domestic bliss and property affairs. Under certain circumstances it can also mean an illicit love affair or a lovers tryst. If lying between King and Queen – a love letter – if with the Ace

of Diamonds an offer of a ring and of with the Eight of Hearts a proposal of marriage.

*Two.* Although this card pertains to love, it has a duality of meaning, depending upon surrounding cards, it can denote a gift – but, if found on the right of a Court Card it means either an engagement, a friend or companionate marriage; but if found on the left, it can mean a warning to avoid marriage with the person the Court Card represents, or a breach of promise suit – particularly if accompanied by three Queens.

*Three.* This is a generally lucky card, meaning success, pleasure and frivolity but it carries a warning of unwise choices. If found on the left of a Court Card, the Sitter is greedy for pleasure and money. The coming success, if near Spades, will be insecure, near Diamonds concerned with money, near Hearts, with love, and near Clubs, with ambition and career. It can also, depending on its position be read as a 'time' card and denote one week in time.

*Four.* This card has different meanings. One is simply a messenger, while depending on its whereabouts it can also mean an unusual link in friendship that will be life-long – as well as anxiety over marriage which could be failing. It denotes sociability but it is also the card of celibacy.

*Five.* Some old authorities believe this card to mean marriage or an engagement. However the accepted meaning is imminent change, also indecision in emotional matters. It can also denote a space of time, e.g. 5 days, weeks or months.

*Six.* This can denote the Past – but usually, it means a talented, balanced person who has great determination, but is over-trusting generous and lazy. With the Love Cards – it can mean courtship or an offer of marriage.

*Seven.* A new emotional venture – with doubts and hesitancy because of broken promises and betrayal from the past. This is

Joy after Sorrow with promised success after initial hesitation. It can also denote a gift – artistic and valuable – but not of money.

*Eight.* This is the love and marriage card particularly with the Ace of Hearts or the Ace of Diamonds. It also denotes a family member or someone with a good heart towards the Sitter, and with certain cards, a legacy, visits and happy journeys.

*Nine.* The happiest card in the pack, the Wish card, stands for desire and talents fulfilled – and its joy and strength lessens the meaning of any negative cards around it.

*Ten.* This card also corrects negative cards around it and has many meanings. It means great affection, good fortune to the house from a wealthy visitor, financial control, returning strength to the invalid, and news of an advantageous marriage. It also means the professional artist actor or musician and brings publicity, glamour and public recognition.

*The Jack.* As in ancient initiation rite he sometimes combined male and female characteristics and was the 'Corn Dolly'. His perversity has come down to us as part of his character. Apart from denoting fair skin, blue or grey eyes and light brown, blond or red hair, he represents a man under 35, high spirited, mischievous, home-loving – but his one fault is he gossips too much.

*Queen.* The Corn Queen in ancient rites, she is beautiful, of medium fair colouring, (as the Jack) loving and faithful. She is never mean or treacherous and, when unattached, attracts men to her like bees to a honeypot. This card often stands for the wife.

*King.* The Corn King in ancient rites – ruddy and fair or greying, he is a man over thirty five, who is powerful in business or the government. He is aristocratic in nature and open handed, talented and affectionate, but his judgement is often emotionally based. Although quick tempered, he is a good and generous husband, and a loyal and steadfast friend.

*Suit of Spades*
*The Ace.* The is only reversal used and the Reader must take great care – as only when reversed does this card mean death, illness, sorrow or loss. When upright it can mean a high building, a government contract, and satisfaction in a difficult achievement. If with the Ten of Spades it means the armed forces or a uniformed person.

*Two.* This is the card of the Traveller or Immigrant, meaning the sudden breaking up of existing conditions, leaving home, a long journey and loss of friends. It can also mean illness but when with business cards – a letter or contract.

*Three.* A quarrel – or tears over interference by others. It can mean failure, haste – restriction and an indefinite period in regard to time.

*Four.* The temporary loss of health or property through the envy and malice of others – troublesome journeys – and disagreements with relatives.

*Five.* The mourning card – it also can mean – depending on surrounding cards – patience finally rewarded and one time partner found after a long search – but it can denote disputes with others.

*Six.* Can mean a voyage – but usually ultimate rewards after detailed work and careful planning – or good luck comes after many reversals. Badly aspected it can mean hindrances to progress.

*Seven.* This card means privation – solitude – lack of money and the loss of true friends through quarrels and warns against jumping to the wrong conclusions. If with the Ten of Diamonds – a money loss.

*Eight.* This is the 'By night' card but it can also mean danger, hidden opposition, snags in contracts or deceit from false friends.

Also it means a roadway or small journey and if with the Nine or Ten of Spades could mean a road accident or a strange bed.

*Nine.* This is the strongest card in the pack. It denotes purity of mind triumphing over all strife, envy, but if with other Spades it can mean slander, malice, financial or domestic failure. If with the Ace of Spades it can mean the death of a dear friend but if the Ace is upright merely the signing of an advantageous legal agreement.

*Ten.* This card can denote a slight sickness, a hospital bed, a long journey with grief at the end, or official or government business, medicine, teaching law and large institutions such as hospitals and universities and hotels.

*Jack.* (In ancient times the Devil's Disciple in the Coven). He is usually a professional man – a lawyer or barrister, or more often a soldier, for his nature is fearless and he has the killer's instinct. He is undisciplined, deceitful and often bad mannered and exploits others for self gain. His colouring is very dark – eyes, skin and hair – and he can represent a foreigner or military man.

*Queen.* (The Maid of the Coven) Fascinating, strong, self reliant, this dark lady makes a wonderful friend, but a bad revengeful enemy, and needs a man as strong to control her. This card often denotes a widow of any colouring or a foreign person.

*King.* (Dark God of the Witches and Lord of the Coven). A dark ambitious man, possibly of military legal or government background – of professional status he is tricky and devious but successful, stubborn and unkind. He makes a bad enemy. This card, as above, can denote a widower or foreigner.

*Suit of Clubs*

*Ace.* Letters – correspondence – documents – contracts concerning work and money – the confirmation of a new lucrative enterprise. This card also means artistic talent brings commercial success. If with the Ten of Spades it can mean sudden news by night and bringing gain (if with the money cards).

*Two.* Children – good friends – association with influential people but it warns the Sitter to keep his or her counsel about future plans for there will be hidden opposition.

*Three.* Economy! This card says 'keep your money in your pocket'. It also, depending upon surrounding cards, can mean a small journey concerning work, or a marriage after a long partnership. Depending on its position – can denote three months in time.

*Four.* Journeys for business purposes, but a darker meaning warns of indiscretion with the spoken word and legal proceedings resulting.

*Five.* The Out of Town Card – either the Sitter comes from a distance or is going on a trip shortly or it denotes news from abroad. It also can mean a wealthy and happy marriage is in the offing but warns of impetuous action which could jeopardise it.

*Six.* The card meaning Gifts or Presents – it also has other meanings – new appointments – harmony in business and political relationship – it holds the hidden potential in either assets or minerals on land that has not been developed.

*Seven.* Solid and substantial success in work is ensured provided the Sitter does not give in half way and that his methods are above board. One hazard for the younger enquirer with this card, is wasting time by dalliance with the opposite sex. This meaning applies only if Court Cards are present.

*Eight.* In both emotional and physical sense this card is fortunate, denoting balance and moderation. It can mean, if with the Seven of Clubs, a new appointment bringing great benefits which will come through the help of a friend. Can also mean a long voyage.

*Nine.* The most fortunate card in the pack, it denotes progress and expansion wherever it appears and softens any negative influences around it. Pertaining to professionalism it can bring fame, publicity and long water journeys.

*Ten.* The expansion and consolidation of Big Business. If with Eight of Hearts – an unexpected inheritance. Journeys – with happy reunions – new successful business interests and ideas – advantageous property dealing – large amounts of money earned – but definitely not in the Pools (this is portrayed by 'Unearned money' in Diamond Suit).

*Jack.* (The Jester of the Coven). A sincere and stable 'nut brown' man, a good friend in time of trouble – he abhors all falsehood and intrigue. His kindness to some might appear as weakness, but he is not in the least weak, as they will find.

*Queen.* (The Seer of the Lodge or Coven). Of medium dark skin and hair and green or hazel eyes, she is spontaneous, lovable, affectionate, but inquisitive – yet she is an excellent guardian of her friends' secrets. She always has money to share and will help the Sitter in small ways. She loves children and this card often stands for the mother.

*King.* (The Soothsayer of the Lodge or Coven). Strong in body and mind, a stalwart friend and companionate husband, he is devoted to social causes and a rock in time of storm. This card often stands for the father.

*Suit of Diamonds*

*Ace.* The ring card when seen with the Ace of Hearts denotes engagement and when with Eight or Nine of Hearts, marriage. It also means an important letter concerning money on its way. If it is with the Nine or Ten of Clubs, there will be a sudden financial uprise through work already completed.

*Two.* Something unexpected – or a secret concerning money –

it denotes partial success only. It can also mean a tragic love affair or erratic undependable source of income is holding the Sitter back.

*Three.* 'Time' card and Trade card – it pertains to lucky 'wheeling and dealing' and represents one month in money matters, pleasure, visits.

*Four.* This is a warning to the Sitter to check on any new project or person he or she has dealing with. It also cautions against neglecting old friends. It can also denote short journeys.

*Five.* The card of a healthy marriage if the Sitter realises that 'honesty pays at all times'.

*Six.* Offers of money – this card warns against financial speculation and also advises caution if the matter of a second marriage is being considered.

*Seven.* This card means a new financial enterprise with a problem attached, which is not insoluble. It also means a gift of money or tickets or fares paid to the Sitter and if seen with other Sevens, the birth of a child.

*Eight.* Can mean a journey which brings new relationships and future happiness, and with Eight of Spades means constant road journeys. It is also the card of Balance, juggling financial skill – material success and a deep spirituality, unselfishness, fairness. The material side of life will never predominate with this Sitter. If near Clubs it denotes smooth steady progress. Can also bring a decision about money.

*Nine.* This is the 'material' wish card – wealth sometimes 'unearned money' and if near Clubs – the cards of Effort – it always means material success – with Ten of Clubs can denote long water journey.

*Ten.* This card brings wealth – but the kind that keeps one in bondage. It is a selfish, shallow card – bringing inherited wealth and a possible lack of spiritual values unless placed with Clubs and Spades which bring it effort and spiritual suffering. It also denotes change both for good and bad in a financial sense.

*Jack.* (The God Hermes in Initiation Rites). Cunning, clever professional man often appearing wealthier than he is – full of charm but insincere.

*Queen.* (The May Queen in Ancient village ceremonies). A shallow restless mercurial woman, a magnet to men, she loves money and managing other people. She has a head for finance, has good principles but is hard and brittle and will always put herself first. This card can also denote the grandmother.

*King.* (The Devouring Sun in Initiation Rites). Artistic, subtle, quick witted, critical, lacking in confidence, with great business acumen, this man can be moody and easily hurt. His confidence needs building up. He never lacks money and often makes it the be all and end all of existence. He can be ruthless.

## SOME RULES WHEN SELECTING COLOURING OF SITTER

Traditionally Diamonds represent the fairest colouring – that of white or freckled skin, blue or grey eyes and blonde or red hair. However, when a person's hair whitens he or she automatically takes the preceding colouring so that if he or she were considered to be a Heart – that is a person with fair skin, blue or grey eyes and brown or light brown hair, he or she would, when grey, become a Diamond. If totally white haired and over 50, even a Club or Spade person becomes a Diamond for the purposes of reading. A Club person possesses light olive skin hazel green or brown eyes and brown or light brown hair. If greying, or even white and still comparatively young, he or she would be represented by a Heart – if over fifty, a Diamond. Spades represent the darkest people, the Mediterranean type, with true olive skins, light, dark brown or black eyes and dark brown or black hair.

There are two things to remember when choosing a Sitter's colouring. First, take in this order – eyes, skin and hair (the natural colour). Secondly, as the Spade Court Cards also represent foreigners, as well as a military man, a widow and widower, it is sometimes wiser to choose Clubs, for a sitter with dark colouring and leave the Spades free.

Also – should your sitter be foreign and very dark, colouring cannot always apply in the reading and you will have to omit them.

## SOME IMPORTANT COMBINATIONS

No card is ever read alone, and as many of the cards have two or three meanings, sometimes contrary, it is only possible to interpret them accurately within the set of cards being studied.

Many of the cards take on a different meaning when combined with others to that accepted in the singular.

The following combinations should be learned. It is a good idea to affix labels to the backs of your cards with these meanings typed or written on them, as there are so many.

*Groups of Cards*

A preponderance of Court Cards always means crowds and company.

Three or more Kings means honours – preferment or a good position for the Sitter.

Three or more Queens means scandal or written publicity about the Sitter.

Three or four Jacks means workmen around the house, the armed forces or police business.

Three or four Aces mean a wonderful new life is in the offing.

Two Queens means company coming.

Two Kings or Jacks, medical or legal help for the Sitter.

Four Tens means good luck financially, three nines, particularly if the nine of Spades is absent brings sudden good fortune and three Sevens always means a birth, either of a person or an enterprise.

*Minor Combinations*

Many of the low numbered cards are used to denote time – e.g. the three of Hearts can mean '3 months, days or weeks' – but sometimes pairs of cards can have a special meaning – a red pair being more fortunate than a black pair.

The Black Aces coming together can pertain to mental conditions, the occult and creative inspiration while the Red Aces together mean happiness through true love.

Whereas the Red Twos can be time cards, they also mean a meeting, but the Black Twos warn against neglect of small details.

The Red Threes are time cards, while the Black Threes warn against lack of patience.

The Red Fours can be time cards but also mean perfection and completion, while the Black Fours warn against Black Magic.

The Red Fives, while time cards, also denote a little used resource of the Sitter bringing good fortune, while the Black Fives counsel the Sitter to examine his business affairs more thoroughly.

The Red Sixes are time cards, and also denote mental or artistic ability, while the Black Sixes denote negativity and the possibility of the Sitter being drained by others.

The Red Sevens denote changes – and time – but the Black Sevens are stumbling blocks to an emotional relationship.

The Red Eights denote Justice but carry a warning of procrastation and the Black Eights denote an intellectual awakening.

The Red Nines are joyful cards with a warning to the Sitter to keep his balance while the Black Nines warn the Sitter to consider carefully what he really wants from life – as his goals are unrealistic.

The Red Tens denote selfless love and are a power for good, while the Black Tens warn against oversensitivity and jealousy.

*Particular Card Combinations*

The Ace of Diamonds with the Three of Hearts: Marriage with a new acquaintance, or within three . . .

The Ace of Diamonds with the Two of Hearts: Affection from someone unknown.

The Ace of Spades with the Ten of Spades: Someone going to prison or been to prison or in prison.

The Ace of Spades with the Nine of Spades: An operation.

The Ace of Spades with the Eight of Spades: An accident.

The Ace of Spades with the Seven of Spades: Signing legal papers.

The Ace of Spades with the Nine of Hearts: Success in legal matters.

The Ace of Spades with the Ace of Clubs: Letter to do with the law.

The Ace of Spades with the Eight of Clubs: Confusion, deception.

The Ace of Spades with the Seven of Clubs: A position with the government.

The Ace of Spades with the Nine of Diamonds: A small windfall.

The Ace of Spades with the Eight of Diamonds: Contracts.

The Ten of Spades with the Eight of Spades: Be careful of an accident to do with transport.

The Ten of Spades with the Eight of Diamonds: Business transactions by night.

The Ten of Spades with the Ten of Hearts: A celebration, a gathering of people.

The Ten of Spades with the Eight of Hearts: Happiness comes by night.

The Ten of Spades with the Seven of Clubs: A change in occupation.

The Eight of Spades with the Ten of Hearts: A place of amusement with a journey out of town.

The Ten of Hearts with the Three of Clubs: A meeting at a social function.

The Ten of Clubs with the Ten of Diamonds: A holiday near water.

The Ten of Clubs with the Seven of Diamonds: Offer of a job (out of town/interstate). Money coming.

The Ten of Clubs with the Nine of Clubs: Journey over deep water.

The Ten of Clubs with the Eight of Clubs: Travel by water, but not necessarily overseas.

The Ten of Diamonds with the Nine of Hearts: Signing of legal documents.

The Ten of Diamonds with the Seven of Hearts: A gift of money, usually by a cheque.

The Nine of Hearts with the Eight of Clubs: Serenity and the achieving of the heart's desire. A direct indication.

The Ace of Diamonds with the Ten of Hearts: A wedding.

The Ace of Diamonds with the Ten of Diamonds: A windfall.

The Ace of Diamonds with the Ten of Spades: Unhappy marriage.

The Ace of Diamonds with the Ten of Clubs: A vacation. Leading to romance. A gift of jewellery from a distance.

The Ace of Diamonds with the Nine of Hearts: The heart's desire to do with love.

The Ace of Diamonds with the Nine of Diamonds: A surprise wedding.

The Ace of Diamonds with the Nine of Spades: Disappointment about romance.

The Ace of Diamonds with the Nine of Clubs: An engagement which will end in marriage.

The Ace of Diamonds with the Eight of Hearts: Rejoicing over happy romance.

The Ace of Diamonds with the Eight of Diamonds: A wealthy marriage.

The Ace of Diamonds with the Eight of Spades: A fiance who travels frequently.

The Ace of Diamonds with the Eight of Clubs: Vexation around a marriage. Vexation around a man who drinks a lot.

The Ace of Diamonds with the Seven of Hearts: A successful marriage.

The Ace of Diamonds with the Seven of Diamonds: An arranged marriage.

The Ace of Diamonds with the Seven of Spades: Separation of a married couple.

The Ace of Diamonds with the Seven of Clubs: For certain romance ends in marriage.

The Ace of Diamonds with the Six of Hearts: News of an engagement.

The Ace of Diamonds with the Four of Hearts: A good marriage.

## THE SIGNIFICANCE OF THE NUMERALS ON THE CARDS

While each card has its own meanings, those carrying the same numerals will share the same influence, according to their suit – some positive, some negative. These underlying meanings are derived from the traditional science of Numerology, and can be used at the end of a Card Reading to give additional information. Often, if the reading seems confusing, they can be used to clarify.

The method is to ask the Sitter either to pick one card at random from the pack, and the numerical meaning is noted – or to pick three cards. If two of those three cards possess the same number, the meaning is reinforced – and if two are red cards, i.e. diamonds or hearts, the result will be lucky. If the numbers all vary, you will have to relate back to your reading to see if their meanings clarify the issue. Two or three black cards would mean that whatever the outcome, hard work and suffering would be experienced first.

*One or Ace.* The number of the individual also means the beginning or the final completion of something and when next to a

Court Card, brings harmony, creative ability and leadership – but warns against domination and egotism.

*Two.* This number is the number of partnership. It can simply denote a period of time i.e. 2 months, 2 days, 2 weeks – a chance meeting. It also denotes a caution or a warning.

*Three.* This number is traditionally lucky, and means revelation, surprise, purification, sympathy.

*Four.* This is the number of completion and the realisation of ambition. It also means consultations.

*Five.* This is a highly spiritual number with a dual meaning. It is always taken as an exhortation to the Sitter to accentuate the positive aspects of his character and become master of his fate. It also represents hidden talents, unsuspected mental powers and deep religious feeling.

*Six.* This too has a dual side. Although it indicates artistic and literary ability – sometimes to genius level – if shown in negative aspect (i.e. with two black cards) it warns against excessive consumption of alcohol and drugs.

*Seven.* Sevens always show new ventures and changes of fortune or residence. They also warn the Sitter to seek for truth and wisdom in order to achieve balance.

*Eight.* To the ancients this number represented the Scales of Justice. They represent a turning point in the Sitter's career and his future will be determined by the right or wrong action. It can bring Justice, Fame and Happiness, but if he is envious of others or broods over the past he will deplete the vital mental energy needed to make progress.

*Nine.* This number always concerns the highest wishes of the Sitter – and can mean realisation or disappointment depending on accompanying cards. If only one card is chosen, the nine of Hearts gives an emotional wish – the nine of Diamonds a money wish. Together they are very lucky. If Clubs: a work project is realised, and if Spades: delays and checks to progress. If a Five of any suit is with any of them, it denotes psychic ability and if preceded by a Seven, a change of wish or objective is advised as something better is awaiting the Sitter.

*Ten.* This represents finality – the end result. The Ten of Hearts denotes great social or artistic activity, the mass media publicity and the theatre. The other Tens pertain to business (Diamonds) Health (Clubs) and officialdom (Spades) and are always lucky.

## METHODS OF READING

### THE SEAL OF SOLOMON

If further clarification is called for, the reader asks the sitter to shuffle again and cut into three packs. After reading the top cards quickly the reader asks the sitter to reshuffle, then deals the cards into five piles, as in a cross with a pack in the centre. Firstly: 'What crowns you', then, below: 'What crosses you'. On the left: 'What faces you', to the right: 'What you turn your back on', and, in the centre: 'What is to yourself'.

During the reading of this combination, the sitter is told that what he will have to turn his back on, or has quite possibly turned his back on, in the recent past will have little bearing on the future, although both could influence decisions. There is a warning implicit in the pack 'What crosses you' for it can sometimes mean unwise and hasty decisions resulting in loss, and is always a future happening. However, 'What you turn your back on' can also carry the seeds of failure because of unwise decisions and often the warning in the former is because of past behaviour

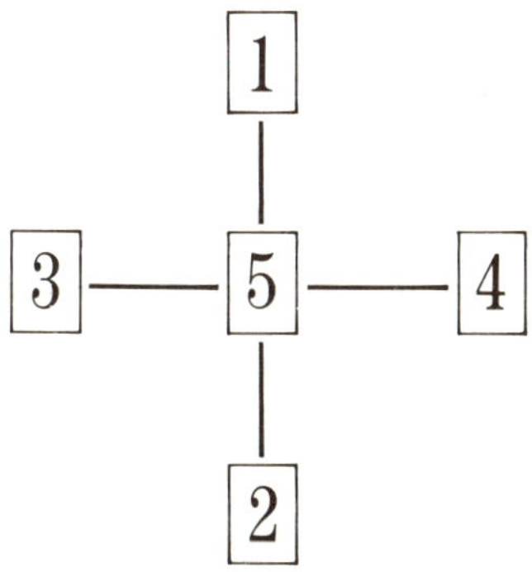


*The Seal of Solomon*

or actions. The three most important packs are 'What is to yourself', which is in the imminent future, leading to 'What faces you and, the overriding pack, 'What crowns you', which should be read as the far future and the result of future efforts. If the sitter's card is found among the cards in 'What crosses you', then it will mean that danger of wrong action will be avoided by his or her presence.

*The Wheel of Fortune*

Another method, using the sitter's representative card in the centre and the cutting of the pack into three as in 'The Star' method is The Wheel of Fortune. Here, the reader lays out nine packs of three cards each, as in Diagram 4, saying, 'Three above you, three below you, three behind you, three before you, three for your house and home, three for your hopes and fears, three for what you don't expect, three for what you do expect and three for what's sure to come.' The remaining cards are not used, but may be called upon if clarification is needed on a particular aspect. In that case, they must be shuffled by the sitter once more before reading.

*The Twenty-One Card Method*

This requires only thirty-three cards and, we take the Two of

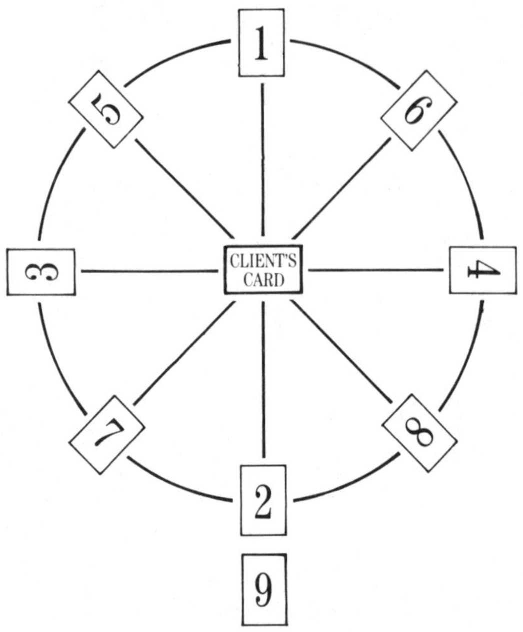


*The Wheel of Fortune*

Hearts to represent the consultant. After shuffling the cards, we deal off eleven and lay them aside, then reshuffle the remaining twenty-two cards. Laying the top card aside for the 'Surprise', we place the consultant's card (the Two of Hearts) anywhere in the pack, then we cut. Putting the two packs together again, we then lay the cards face up in a straight line, placing the surprise face down below the cards in the centre of the row. The reader now reads the cards as they run, noting the cards around the consultant's card carefully, then turns up the surprise. If it is near the sitter's card it will foretell imminent happenings, if further away it will take longer and, developing upon its suit and meaning, it will override or support or detract from the reading. The reader now collects the cards to be reshuffled and cut into three piles, the top card being taken away. This is done three times, so that there are now three cards for a 'Surprise'. If Hearts predominate in these three cards, then there will be happiness and felicity around domestic conditions. If Diamonds, prosperity coming to the sitter; if Clubs, then a successful business project. Spades are a warning to watch health and personal concerns closely.

Another method of card reading is to use only the Aces, Kings, Queens, Jacks, Tens, Nines, Eights and Sevens.

Shuffle the 32 cards and deal, counting out one, two, three, four, five and six. Then put the seventh card aside. Count six again – discard them and add the seventh card to the first card you put aside. Repeat this until you have only four cards in your hand.

Count these and pick up the Discards again, saying One – Two – Three – Four – Five – Six – Seven – place the seventh card with the special cards and continue in this fashion, using the Discarded cards until you have 12 cards in your selected pile.

Notice whether red or black cards preponderate and read any combinations. The cards are not read one by one – but count to seven – then another seven from left to right and read these two together always going back to the beginning on the first card from the left – and ending on 12th or last card in the set-out.

To get additional information – couple the cards, reading the first and 12th – second and 11th – third and tenth – and so on until the last pair – the 6th and 7th have been read in conjunction.

## SIMPLE CARD READING METHODS

### THE SEVEN PACKS

Firstly, all cards under the denomination of Seven must be taken from the pack, retaining four Sevens, Eights, Nines, Tens and the Court cards, plus the Aces. This makes a pack of thirty two cards. Now the sitter shuffles the cards well and cuts once. The reader picks the two packs up, reads the top two cards, noting their meanings, then, placing the two packs together in the same order, deals the cards out one by one to form seven heaps, four in the top row and three in the bottom. The seven packs represent 'Self' (the sitter), 'Home', 'Friend', 'Wish', 'What you do expect', 'What you don't expect', and 'What's sure to come true'.

*Diagram 1: The Seven Packs*

1 2 3 4
5 6 7

Some packs will only have four cards while others have five. When reading, first place the sitter in the appropriate suit, according to his or her colouring. For Hearts, take fair skin and blue or grey eyes together with light brown hair; for Clubs, light or dark brown hair, green or hazel eyes and mid-brown skin colouring; for Diamonds, red or flaxen hair, light blue eyes and the fairest of skin colouring. While the Spades suit must correspond with black or blue-black hair and black or very dark brown eyes set in an olive complexion. If a person's hair has been very dark and is now greying, the corresponding colour will drop one tone (Clubs) while Hearts and Clubs, when white, will often drop to Diamonds, depending on their age.

As there are less cards for females than males in the pack it is often the practice of card readers to take the Queen of Hearts as the significator no matter what the sitter's colouring and, if married, the King as her husband. This may be a more reliable method for beginners, as there is often confusion as to the Court Cards, when grouped meaning professional men, not particularly personal friends of the sitter, and the Spade Court cards can often pertain to moral qualities rather than actual people.

Having noted the two cards turned up at the cut, as they will have an overall bearing upon the entire reading, then the reader studies each pack in turn. Firstly, note the preponderance of one suit, if any, combinations of Court cards and the position of the 'wish card' – the Nine of Hearts. Each card must be studied in relation to the cards before and after it. When the reading is concluded, then the sitter is asked to shuffle and spread the pack out fanwise across the table, while wishing in general terms for what he most desires and to pick seven cards. It must be impressed upon the sitter that to make a wish specific is limiting. For instance, he must never ask for money but rather for those conditions which will bring him abundance, freedom from debt, or the ability to provide comforts for his dear ones. The seven cards divide into two sets of three with the fourth (or middle) card being the decisive element of the reading of the wish.

## THE MYSTIC STAR

The reader chooses the representative card for the sitter and places it upwards in the centre of the table. The reader then shuffles the pack well so that it is impregnated with her personality and her emotional state. Then she makes three random cuts and places the packs face downwards on the table. This is traditionally cut by the left hand for it is believed that the 'hand of the devil' rules the unconscious and is the true motivation of our behaviour. The reader then turns up to the top cards of the three packs, reading these cards separately then in combination, which will give a general indication as to whether the reading will be generally favourable or unlucky. The three packs are then gathered together and the sitter is asked to reshuffle them. When this is done, the reader makes the figure of 'The Star' as is shown in Diagram 2. The cards are laid anticlockwise, one card at each point and in that precise order. The reader then hands the remaining cards to the sitter and asks her to place two additional cards in the order he has illustrated on each point of the Star so that there will

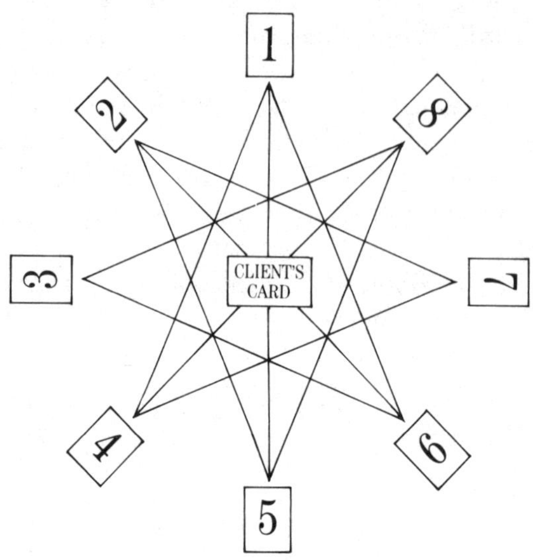


*The Mystic Star*

finally be three cards at each point, all lying face downwards. Turning each three up in an anti-clockwise direction, the reader then studies each pile and finally gives a complete summary when every card is disclosed.

*Chapter Eight*

# The Astrological Horoscope

The 52 cards in the pack correspond to the weeks in a year
The 4 Suits represent the 4 seasons
Each suit has 13 cards to correspond with each quarter
The 12 courtcards govern the signs of the Zodiac e.g.

ARIES—King of Hearts
TAURUS—Queen of Diamonds
GEMINI—Jack of Clubs
CANCER—King of Spades
LEO—Queen of Hearts
VIRGO—Jack of Diamonds
LIBRA—King of Clubs
SCORPIO—Queen of Spades
SAGGITARIUS—Jack of Hearts
CAPRICORN—King of Diamonds
AQUARIUS—Queen of Clubs
PISCES—Knave of Spades

Each sign is traditionally divided into 3 decanates of approximately 10 days each decanate. The numbered suit cards excluding the ace – are nine in each suit. These are divided into three groups of three. So – the 4–7–10 of each suit are associated with the King of that suit, e.g.:

King of Hearts with 4–7–10 of Hearts
King of Diamonds with 4–7–10 of Diamonds
King of Clubs with 4–7–10 of Clubs
King of Spades with 4–7–10 of Spades
The 2–5–8 of each suit are associated with their Queen
Queen of Hearts with 2–5–8 of Hearts
Queen of Diamonds with 2–5–8 of Diamonds
Queen of Clubs with 2–5–8 of Clubs
Queens of Spades with 2–5–8 of Spades
The 3–6–9 are associated with the Jack
Jack of Hearts with 3–6–9 of Hearts
Jack of Diamonds with 3–6–9 of Diamonds
Jack of Clubs with 3–6–9 of Clubs
Jack of Spades with 3–6–9 of Spades

## RULER OF THE DECANATES

| Suit | Sign | 1st | 2nd Decanate | 3rd | Ruler |
|---|---|---|---|---|---|
| Hearts | Aries | 4 | 7 | 10 | King |
| Diamonds | Taurus | 2 | 5 | 8 | Queen |
| Clubs | Gemini | 3 | 6 | 9 | Jack |
| Spades | Cancer | 4 | 7 | 10 | King |
| Hearts | Leo | 2 | 5 | 8 | Queen |
| Diamonds | Virgo | 3 | 6 | 9 | Jack |
| Clubs | Libra | 4 | 7 | 10 | King |
| Spades | Scorpio | 2 | 5 | 8 | Queen |
| Hearts | Sagittarius | 3 | 6 | 9 | Jack |
| Diamonds | Capricorn | 4 | 7 | 10 | King |
| Clubs | Aquarius | 2 | 5 | 8 | Queen |
| Spades | Pisces | 3 | 6 | 9 | Jack |

Each courtcard relates to a specific factor in the Horoscope reading.

The King Represents:
The sun and the spirit – positive male principle – the father – creative energy – vital forces – and has affinity with the sun or circle.
The Queen Represents:
The moon and the soul – the mother – the passive negative female principle – the preserving nurturing power – functional activity and has affinity with the moon or semicircle.
The Jack Represents:
The earth – child of either sex – the body – neutral forces – matter and materialism and has affinity with the cross.

The threefold elemental division of the Signs is denoted as The Kings and their three associated cards represent:
Cardinal Signs
The Queen and her three associated cards represent:
Fixed Signs
The Jack and his three associated cards represent:
Mutable Signs
These three – King, Queen and Jack represent the threefold force, Spirit Soul, Body and Mother, Father Child.
The King represents Action
The Queen represents Determination
The Jack represents the 'thought' or mind of the Enquirer.

## THE ELEMENTS AND TRIPLICITIES

The Four Suits also denote the four elements and the four triplicities dividing the twelve signs symbolizing Spirit – Body – Mind and Soul.

*Fire Sign*
Hearts – Aries – Leo – Sagittarius – governing spiritual nature, higher emotions and Summer Period June 22–September 23.

*Earth Sign*
Diamonds – Taurus – Virgo – Capricorn governing physical nature, material aspects and Spring Period March 21–June 22.

*Air Sign*
Clubs – Gemini – Libra – Aquarius – govern mental natures and intellectual pursuits and Autumn Period September 23–December 22.

*Water sign*
Spades – Cancer – Scorpio – Pisces – Psychic nature – mediumistic ability – Winter Period December 22–March 21.

## THE SUIT CARDS

*The Ace*, when it appears in the Horoscope is taken to be the 'PART OF FORTUNE'.
*The Two*: has an affinity with URANUS – so denotes the unexpected event.
*The Three*: this card, being a 'time' card relates directly to the Tenth House – OR MERIDIAN – (The House of Career).
*The Four*: is connected with the 8 – and relates to Third House.
*The Five*: is connected with the Second House (Money – material benefits).
*The Six*: has strong connections with Seventh House (it is ruled by Venus) so it relates to offers and proposals.
*The Seven*: is connected with Eleventh House – ruling favours and presents.
*The Eight*: relates to the Ninth House.
*The Nine*: relates to the Fifth House which rules luck and speculation.

*The Ten*: is ruled by Jupiter and always denotes something expansive, large and generous.

Should any of these number cards fall in their designated Houses in the Horoscope Reading – they heighten the significance of those concerns ruled by the Houses.

*The Basic Meaning of the Numbers*

*The Ace* – is the Personal Card – denoting personal wishes and inner desires.
*The two*: always unexpected events.
*The Three*: Time – period or age.
*The Four*: Short journeys – communications.
*The Five*: Material gains and benefits.
*The Six*: Offers and Proposals.
*The Seven*: Things received, given.
*The Eight*: Long distance travelling.
*The Nine*: This represents Luck in each suit.
*The Ten*: All important financial matters and in profession – property, talent and ability, work contracts, legal papers.

*Card Meanings for Horoscope Readings*

The card meanings hitherto given are simplified for the purpose of laying a Horoscope. The general significance of each card, coupled with the various subjects ruled by the twelve Houses of the Zodiac will allow much diversity in interpretation and will depend on the Reader's own intuition.

### Diamonds

Diamonds represent financial transactions – money – speculation – investments – gold – silver – jewellery – household goods and clothing. They bring success in those matters which are governed by the house in which they appear in the horoscope.

*King*: Man (over 25) of very fair colouring (or white or grey haired) – light eyes – affectionate – sometimes fickle – connected with financial concerns.
*Queen*: Woman (over 25) of same colouring – (red or blonde or white hair) sometimes shallow – sociable and pleasure loving.
*Jack*: A young very fair person (under 25) of either sex – sociable – pleasure loving.
*Ten*: Unearned money – legacies – financial benefits through others.
*Nine*: Financial luck or surprise – unexpected gains.
*Eight*: Journeys – either business or pleasure – related to money.
*Seven*: Gift of money – banknotes – fare given or tickets sent.
*Six*: Business offers bringing money – offer of money.
*Five*: Health – wealth – material increase.
*Four*: Short journeys connected with money.
*Three*: One month in financial affairs, visits for pleasure.
*Two*: Unexpected development or a secret concerning money.
*Ace*: The 'Ring' card – meaning marriage but also wealth.

## Hearts

Hearts are concerned with courtship, marriage, love, birth of children, social matters – friendship – house and home – and represents success in the creative arts and in those matters governed by the 'house' they will occupy in the horoscope reading.

*King*: Man of medium fair colouring – popular, affectionate and respected. Often artistically talented.
*Queen*: Woman of similar colouring, loving, constant, warm hearted and devoted to family.
*Knave*: A young person or child of between colours. Reliable, home-loving, obedient.
*Ten*: Friends, pleasurable activities, associations, public gatherings and entertainment, social intercourse.
*Nine*: The wish card, hopes and dreams realised – career and work ambitions achieved.

*Eight*: Happy pleasurable visits and journeys. The marriage or family card.
*Seven*: A gift of something either useful and of value or artistic and treasured.
*Six*: Marriage offer – courtship – meeting with other sex.
*Five*: Engagement, pleasure, denotes a child.
*Four*: Social invitations – or frustration in marriage.
*Three*: One week in visits – pleasures.
*Two*: A present – not money. A reunion or reconciliation of some kind.
*Ace*: The home – the house or property, family concerns.

**Clubs**

Clubs are related to work, business, profession – position in life, honour reputation, marriage, partnership, the countryside, worldly success and artistic talent (more with the hands than the head – such as painting, sculpting etc). They denote success in all matters governed by the Houses in which they fall in the horoscope.

*King*: A man of mid brown colouring and hazel, green or light brown eyes. A prosperous and respected business man or professional, generous and tolerant who is happier in the country than the city.
*Queen*: A woman of like colouring, industrious, ingenious, organised and capable. She loves children and animals, her home, country pursuits, and is loving and loyal to her friends and kin.
*Knave*: A 'nut brown' young person, clever, industrious, talented and reliable.
*Ten*:Success in profession, position or vocation, and good business transactions.
*Eight*: Long journeys to foreign countries by sea or air of long trips to do with business.
*Seven*: This means a solid and substantial gain – according to the house position.

*Six*: A business appointment – can be an offer or an actual position.
*Five*: Foreign correspondence – news received from abroad.
*Four*: Many small journeys for business purposes.
*Three*: This card means 3 months in any matter relating to the 'House' it occupies.
*Two*: Help from influential, kind and honourable friends.
*Ace*: Letters – correspondence contracts, agreements, documents.

**Spades**

The spades denote the challenges of Life – the trials of sickness, losses, bereavement, difficulties, hurdles, troubles which beset us all. They show these in differing aspects, according to where they are placed in the Houses.

*King*: A man of 'Latin' colouring with dark brown eyes, olive skin and black or dark brown hair. He is a man of hasty temper, stubborn, argumentative and basically a fighter. This card can also represent a foreigner.
*Queen*: A woman of similar colouring who, if your enemy, can be jealous, vengeful and unscrupulous, but can be a wonderful if somewhat dominating friend. This card also denotes the widow.
*Jack*: A young person of either sex – of the same colouring – who needs guidance because he or she is in bad company or because of their reckless extravagance – both in money and behaviour.
*Ten*: Difficulties, obstacles and losses – but this card also denotes work for the government, hotels, hospitals and large corporations, as well as meaning wearing a uniform of some kind, e.g. the armed forces or police.
*Nine*: Trouble through others; slander and malice bringing suffering – but it also can denote a delay or a legal paper signed.
*Eight*: Possible danger on a roadway or a hospital bed – or simply a journey or removal of home.

*Seven*: Anxiety over money or a period of privation. It also denotes a new start clouded by self-doubt and indecision.
*Six*: a stalemate in business affairs or temporary hindrance to progress.
*Five*: The 'quarrel' card – brings unhappiness in dealing with others.
*Four*: Sad or troublesome journeys or family disagreements.
*Three*: An indefinite factor in regard to time or uncertainty.
*Two*: Loss, tears and sorrow. A removal of some kind – but this can also mean signing important papers.
*Ace*: Pointing downwards, this card means bereavement or grave illness – but reversed it means signing important papers in a high building.

## The Significance of Each Card in the 12 Houses

*Diamonds*  *The King of Diamonds in the Houses*
HOUSE
FIRST Very fair, tall man, kind, affectionate, somewhat fickle – connected with financial concerns such as money – banking – stocks and shares. THIS CARD ALSO DENOTES THE FATHER.
SECOND Gain through banks, stocks, shares. Luck with fair people – meeting a speculative, enterprising fair man.
THIRD A tall fair male relative plays an important part in the enquirer's life – or wealthy relations – or journeys in connection with money.
FOURTH Wealthy stable home, particularly the father. A successful winding up of financial ventures.
FIFTH Several male children – usually successful – but this also warns of the gambling instinct.
SIXTH Can mean an employer of labour but usually denotes the loss of health through pursuit of wealth.
SEVENTH In a woman's horoscope this means a wealthy husband – in a male's – it means either a good business partnership or a successful marriage.

EIGHTH A gain by legacy from a male member of the family or an easy end with good attention and nursing.
NINTH Foreign travel brings financial reward, or a generous person who gives freely to hospitals and religious concerns.
TENTH A person holding a prominent position in a large financial company or institution – a financial magnate.
ELEVENTH Friends among wealthy people – help financial ambitions.
TWELFTH Restriction through lack of money. Too much emphasis on money-making.

## Diamonds The Queen

HOUSE
FIRST Fair woman – vain, fickle – society-loving and wealthy.
THIS CARD ALSO REPRESENTS THE MOTHER.
SECOND This denotes extravagance and vanity and is a warning to save money for the future.
THIRD Journeys for pleasure – holidays.
FOURTH A wealthy mother, stable environment and good financial position in old age.
FIFTH Female children – fickleness in love – fond of dancing and social pursuits.
SIXTH Home comforts needed. Health can be affected by too much pleasure-seeking. A warning of waste.
SEVENTH For a male enquirer this denotes a wealthy spouse. For a female enquirer it means public recognition and prestigious partnerships.
EIGHTH Gain through will or legacy from female member of family.
NINTH Foreign travel or involvement with church affairs.
TENTH Honours for a female or prestigious career.
ELEVENTH Lots of female friends (this means the same for either male or female).
TWELFTH Scandal through women or enmity from women.

*Diamonds The Jack*

HOUSE

FIRST Pleasure-loving, fashion-conscious extravagant young fair man or woman.

SECOND Extravagance and prodigality in money matters.

THIRD Changeable, unreliable – unable to concentrate on studies.

FOURTH Restless and unsettled home life – makes this young person unreliable.

FIFTH The gambler card – a warning not to speculate.

SIXTH Unsatisfactory progress in work area because health is affected by over indulgences.

SEVENTH Marriage to younger person – often a mistake.

EIGHTH Passing anxiety over partner's wealth.

NINTH Restless enquiring subject gains through travel.

TENTH Many changes and uncertainty in occupation.

ELEVENTH Surrounded by false friends.

TWELFTH Petty jealousies and possible scandal.

*The Ten*

FIRST Similar to King of Diamonds.

SECOND Good earning potential – and business success.

THIRD Financial gain and short journeys brought about by using mental abilities.

FOURTH Gain by legacy.

FIFTH Success through investments and also through children.

SIXTH Gain through a good employee or intermediary.

SEVENTH For a female especially – a successful wealthy marriage.

EIGHTH Gain through will or legacy, and through marriage.

NINTH Foreign affairs and travel bring gain.

TENTH A good well paying position.

ELEVENTH Bcncfits through wealthy friends.

TWELFTH Very little opposition or enemies in life.

*The Nine of Diamonds*

The luck card – the nine always brings unexpected gains and pleasant surprises in all matters governed by the House in the horoscope.

*The Eight of Diamonds*

FIRST Similar to the Queen.

SECOND Travel brings financial reward.

THIRD Similar to above.

FOURTH Many removals and change of residence.

FIFTH Numerous pleasurable trips.

SIXTH Remunerative employment brings much travelling.

SEVENTH This, for a male enquirer, means a successful marriage.

EIGHTH Partnership affairs bring journeys and much activity.

NINTH Foreign countries become important to business and financial concerns – resulting in much travel.

TENTH A profession or occupation brings many new scenes and new faces.

ELEVENTH Friends made all round the world.

TWELFTH Losses by theft while travelling – difficulties – caution against prejudice towards other cultures.

*The Seven of Diamonds*

The Seven is purely a money-card. It signifies financial gain, gifts, tickets or fares paid, etc., in relation to those concerns governed by the Houses in the horoscope.

*The Six of Diamonds*

This card, although also a money card relates purely to business and financial concerns – so, in the fourth House it would denote houses and property, while if in the fifth it would denote such things as stocks and shares.

*The Five of Diamonds*

This card is related to The Queen. It denotes material benefits and general success in all matters, affected by the House it occupies. It is a good card for health – particularly in the First and Sixth house.

*The Four of Diamonds*
The Four has relation to the King and has the same meaning, but is a lesser degree, as the 8 of Diamonds which relates to journeys connected with money.

*The Three of Diamonds*
This card is most significant in the directional part of the horoscope and means that matters governed by the Houses in which it is placed come to fruition in one month.

*The Two of Diamonds*
The mystery of secret or hidden things, this card often denotes the unexpected in relation to those concerns governing the Houses in which it is placed.

*The Ace*
The Ace is an important card and always signifies money and wealth.
FIRST A wealthy generous person.
SECOND A good source of money all through life although inclined to extravagance.
THIRD Many journeys – generosity to family nd friends.
FOURTH A wealthy environment – a good home.
FIFTH Successful children – gain by speculation.
SIXTH A good employer and honest staff.
SEVENTH A wealthy partner or successful marriage.
EIGHT Gain by will and legacy through marriage partner.
NINTH Wealth through science or religion – success through forcign travel.
TENTH Financial power – very important public position.
ELEVENTH Success through wealthy friends or backers.

TWELFTH This card acts as a safeguard against negative influences and brings protection.

## Influence of Hearts in the Twelve Houses

*The King of Hearts in the Houses*

FIRST Medium fair man: artistic, talented, popular and respected. A good father.

SECOND Money through art – music etc. A comfortable standard of living.

THIRD Benefits from a male relative – close family ties.

FOURTH Harmonious and happy domestic life. Peace in old age.

FIFTH Sons who bring credit to their father.

SIXTH A warning of health damage through excess. It also means hard-working honourable employees.

SEVENTH In a female horoscope this means a good husband. Much happiness in marriage. In a male, a beneficial partnership with a mid-brown man over 35.

EIGHTH Gain by will or legacy or through a marriage. A happy old age.

NINTH Happiness and pleasure derived from travel and journeys.

TENTH High social position. A justice or magistrate – great popularity.

ELEVENTH Many highly placed friends.

TWELFTH Very few misfortunes or enemies in life.

*The Queen of Hearts*

FIRST A kind hearted good hostess. She is fond of home and children. Often musically or artistically talented – sometimes a professional in artistic field.

SECOND Money gained through profession to do with art, drama or music.

THIRD Affectionate family – journeys for art or pleasure.

FOURTH Loving, wealthy and artistic mother and background – much happiness in later years.
FIFTH Female children with artistic talents who gain distinction.
SIXTH Domestic happiness, but a warning of over-indulgence.
SEVENTH To a man – a marriage of social consequence. To a woman – she will be a good wife.
EIGHTH Gain by will or legacy through the female line. A peaceful old age.
NINTH A religious, mystical bent – or foreign travel to do with professional activities.
TENTH Musical and artistic success and work. Great popularity.
ELEVENTH Realisation of a dream – many influential female friends.
TWELFTH Female jealousy or envy in musical or artistic circles.

*The Knave of Hearts*
FIRST Clever, reliable, talented and industrious young person of either sex with mid-brown colouring and light eyes.
SECOND A liking for fashionable dress. Great success in money matters.
THIRD Closeness with family – particularly brothers. A clever and talented young person who will undertake many short journeys in the course of his/her work.
FOURTH Stable home environment – much domestic happiness.
FIFTH Much artistic creative success achieved by children.
SIXTH Honest and hard working employees. A warning of over-work.
SEVENTH A happy and successful marriage to someone younger.
EIGHTH Gain through marriage, will or legacy.
NINTH Travel to do with employment or art.
TENTH An important but subordinate position in an artistic field – such as drama, art or music.

ELEVENTH Many young talented artistic friends.
TWELFTH Not many sorrows in life – but jealousy from young people.

*The Ten of Hearts*
FIRST Similar to King of Hearts.
SECOND Much pleasure and profit through association with artistic people.
THIRD Many pleasurable visits and journeys to friends and family.
FOURTH Much family entertaining and jollity. A happy retirement.
FIFTH Large family – gifted, artistic, children.
SIXTH Home comforts, help in the home. Warning of over-indulgence in the pleasurable round.
SEVENTH Domestic felicity. A happy marriage.
EIGHTH Gain through inheritance by marriage partner.
NINTH Long distance travel brings happiness. Deeply religious nature.
TENTH Prestige, honour and success in chosen profession.
ELEVENTH Many happy friendships.
TWELFTH Very few sorrows in life – very little jealousy or enmity.

*The Nine of Hearts*
The nine is the card of fulfilment. The querent realises all his dreams in all the aspects governed by the House of the Card horoscope in which it is placed.

*The Eight of Hearts*
FIRST Similar to the Queen of Hearts
SECOND Money earned through pleasure or art.
THIRD Harmonious relationships with friends or relatives.
FOURTH Hospitality in the home gives great pleasure.
FIFTH Much to do with children or young adults in life.

SIXTH Success in employ of others – a reliable worker.
SEVENTH A good wife or husband. Much married happiness.
EIGHTH Gain by legacy – a peaceful end to life.
NINTH Travel brings happiness.
TENTH Good position involves much travelling.
ELEVENTH Social popularity.
TWELFTH Kindness to the afflicted. Much voluntary work in hospitals and institutions.

*The Seven of Hearts*

The Seven is the Gift Card. It does not relate to money. It denotes presents, gifts, and offers governed by the concerns of the House in which it is placed. For instance, in the Second House – it would denote: jewellery – in the Third: books, in the Fourth: house property – the Eighth: legacies or bequests and in the Tenth: professional offers.

*The Six of Hearts*

This card denotes social affairs, courtship – engagement – offers of marriage and is read in accordance with its position in the Card Horoscope.

*The Five of Hearts*

This card merely denotes pleasure and happiness arising from the matters ruled by the House in which it appears. It is good for marriage when it falls in the Seventh House and for children when found in the Fifth.

*The Four of Hearts*

This card is related to the King and has the same meanings as the 8 of Hearts, but in a lesser degree.

*The Three of Hearts*

This card represents One Week.

*The Two of Hearts*
This is also a gift card, like the seven, but denotes smaller benefits.

*The Ace of Hearts in the Houses*
An important card – denoting happiness, pleasure and sociability.

FIRST A kind and affectionate person.

SECOND Valuable and artistic possessions. Great happiness.

THIRD The artistic gift and creative ability – closeness between brothers and sisters.

FOURTH Attachment to parents

FIFTH Fondness for children – a large family.

SIXTH Good health and domestic comfort.

SEVENTH Well connected marriage partner – successful union.

EIGHTH Considerable inheritance.

NINTH Residence abroad and successful foreign travel.

TENTH Prominent position in artistic profession.

ELEVENTH Wealthy patrons and friends.

TWELFTH Few restrictions – no real opposition.

## The Influence of the Clubs in the Twelve Houses

*The King of Clubs in the Houses*
FIRST A brown haired, hazel, green or brown eyed man – trustworthy, prosperous, and a good businessman.

SECOND Professional and business activities bring financial rewards.

THIRD Keen mind – clever in business. Possible talent for law or writing.

FOURTH Clever, cultured parents. Possible professional or business background.

FIFTH Clever children, particularly sons.

SIXTH Professional employees bring satisfaction.

SEVENTH For a woman – marriage to highly successful professional man or business man. For a man – public recognition and material rewards.

EIGHTH Partnership brings public acclaim and rewards.

NINTH Foreign travel important to success. Denotes an upright honourable man.

TENTH High professional status, i.e. – lawyer, surgeon or managing director.

ELEVENTH Many distinguished friends of all classes.

TWELFTH Magistrate, judge or prison dignitary.

*The Queen*

FIRST 'Nut-brown' woman talented, industrious – a lover of home and children. A nature lover.

SECOND Financial gain through business or domestic concerns.

THIRD A clever talented person – author, teacher, lecturer etc.

FOURTH Many early opportunities – a capable, business-like organiser. A good stable home and environment. A good mother.

FIFTH Children – often female. Very talented and successful.

SIXTH A good employer – successful work with women subordinates. Home comforts.

SEVENTH For a man a very successful marriage with a talented wife. For a woman – public gain.

EIGHTH Gain through female line.

NINTH Travel for professional gain. A deep religious sense.

TENTH A high position or professional career for a female.

ELEVENTH Many good friends among talented high-powered women.

TWELFTH Some jealousy from other women.

*The Knave of Clubs*

FIRST Young nut brown person of either sex – with good business instincts and business ability.

SECOND Money earned through clerical or commercial work.

THIRD An agent, bookseller, tutor, salesman with good mental abilities.

FOURTH Good learning opportunities in early life through clever or industrious parents.
FIFTH Several clever hard working children.
SIXTH Good relations with subordinates or employees.
SEVENTH Marriage to young partner who is talented and commercially minded.
EIGHTH Partnership or co-workers bring benefits.
NINTH Skill in science and imparting knowledge – and successful travel.
TENTH Legal and commercial success.
ELEVENTH Many business acquaintances – mostly young.
TWELFTH Petty annoyance – mainly through scandal and gossip.

*The Ten of Clubs*
This card denotes business transactions, promotions, and work relating to whichever House it occupies.

*The Nine of Clubs*
This is similar to the Ten of Clubs – denoting success and expansion in business, profession and commerce relating to those matters governed by the house in which it appears.

*The Eight of Clubs*
The denotes journeys and foreign travel, affecting the relevant House in which it is found.

*The Seven of Clubs*
This means something solid and substantial given or received – such as a stock and share certificate – a partnership etc. – depending on its House position.

*The Six of Clubs*
This is a most fortunate card which is associated with new work – a new post – a new business offer of a responsible kind which

will enhance the reputation and increase the earnings – according to where it is found in the horoscope.

*The Five of Clubs*
This pertains to letters and correspondence of a commercial nature, depending on its House position.

*The Four of Clubs*
A good card for a male enquirer. It means travelling for professional, business or commercial matters, the nature of which depending upon where it is found in the Houses. It is like the Eight of Clubs but its effect is not as powerful.

*The Three of Clubs*
This card represents three months in all matters pertaining to the House in which it falls.

*The Two of Clubs*
This denotes the unexpected element. It always brings good luck with it, good friends and favourably-disposed people of influence who will assist the enquirer and relates to the concerns of the House in which it falls.

*The Ace of Clubs*
It is always connected with documents, contracts – books, signatures – lease, deeds and other legal papers.
FIRST A clever and discreet person. A writer, lawyer, or commercial manager.
SECOND Money gained through writing, legal or business affairs.
THIRD A commercial traveller – an agent – a collector.
FOURTH Many changes in home life. Very active life.
FIFTH Investor, speculator. Documents relating to these.
SIXTH Under manager, chief clerk, personal assistant.
SEVENTH Professional gain and prestige. Public success. A good card for marriage – both male and female.

EIGHTH Legal documents connected with wills, probate, bequests.
NINTH Literary and scientific work – with foreign connections.
TENTH Legal, literary, or commercial pre-eminence.
ELEVENTH Papers concerning companies, associations, societies.
TWELFTH Correspondence, papers, letters of a secret and confidential nature.

## The Influence of the Spades in the Twelve Houses

*The King of Spades in the Houses*
FIRST Very dark man, determined – persistent ambitious and struggling. A stubborn fighter. Also a foreigner or man in uniform.
SECOND Difficulties and losses in financial affairs.
THIRD Difficult relationship with family and relatives particularly one brother or sister.
FOURTH Father not well disposed to enquirer or unhappy memories of childhood – difficult early years.
FIFTH Children a disappointment. Gambling losses.
SIXTH Unsatisfactory health. Deception from subordinates.
SEVENTH If a woman – an elderly husband. If a man – danger of public opposition.
EIGHTH Trouble and disillusionment over legacies.
NINTH Hasty temper – irreligious person – travel difficulties.
TENTH Warning against over-spending – could bring bankruptcy.
ELEVENTH Many heartbreaks through false friends. Bitterness through failure.
TWELFTH Elderly people oppose hopes and wishes. Danger of restriction or confinement.

*The Queen of Spades*
FIRST The foreigner or widow card – this card also represents a

very dark, domineering, powerful and determined woman, who when crossed can be unscrupulous and revengeful.

SECOND Waste, carelessness and extravagance in money matters brings impoverishment.

THIRD Bad feeling between family members. Malice and misfortune through a female relative.

FOURTH Poor early home conditions. Mother left a widow early in life. Privation in old age.

FIFTH A daughter who causes much sorrow. Trouble through children.

SIXTH Delicate health. Untrustworthy subordinates.

SEVENTH To a male – marriage to a widow or older female. To a woman – enmity from women.

EIGHTH Losses and difficulties with wills.

NINTH An unfavourable card for travel. A hypocritical, bad tempered woman.

TENTH Danger or scandal in business or vulgar pursuits.

ELEVENTH Dangerous friends – enmity from women.

TWELFTH Many restrictions – secret enemies – warning against promiscuous behaviour.

*The Jack of Spades*

FIRST A very dark complexioned youth or girl in danger of being led astray by worthless companions.

SECOND No ability to earn or keep money. A warning against extravagance.

THIRD Rivalry between relations. Few if any brothers or sisters.

FOURTH Many drawbacks in early life. Poor environment.

FIFTH Much sorrow caused by one child – possibly male.

SIXTH Poor health – dishonest workmates or employees.

SEVENTH Unhappy marital state. One partner too young.

EIGHTH Loss through trickery or theft.

NINTH Danger while travelling. Lack of religious faith.

TENTH False reports and scandal. Unemployment.

ELEVENTH Trouble through undesirable acquaintances.
TWELFTH Danger of imprisonment through rash and reckless conduct.

*The Ten of Spades*
This card denotes losses, misfortunes, difficulties and obstacles. In whatever sphere it is found it has the exact opposite influence to the Ten of Hearts.

*The Nine of Spades*
FIRST A weak indecisive negative person – not physically strong.
SECOND Theft and loss through others.
THIRD Malice from family or neighbours.
FOURTH Early bereavement and poverty. A bad start to life.
FIFTH Delicate children – much worry with them.
SIXTH Plagued by ill health and malicious subordinates.
SEVENTH Scandal in married life – or celibacy preferred.
EIGHTH Lingering or chronic illness or suffering. Losses.
NINTH Frustration in travel.
TENTH Loss of position through malice and evil actions of others.
ELEVENTH Damage to reputation – through falsehood.
TWELFTH Restriction and suffering caused by others.

*The Eight of Spades*
This card has a particular connection with removals, journeys and travel and if placed in the FIRST, THIRD OF NINTH House denotes possible disasters and warns agains travelling.

*The Seven of Spades*
This card notes anxiety over lack of money, privation and unemployment.
FIRST Poverty or poor circumstances bring constant anxiety.
SECOND Lack of money.

THIRD A despondent person or relative.
FOURTH Deprivation in childhood.
FIFTH Children are a constant drain on resources.
SIXTH Indifferent health – caused by tension.
SEVENTH Lack of money prevents marriage.
EIGHTH Worry about the future.
NINTH Lack of money affects religious matters and restricts travel.
TENTH Ill paid position – unreliable work.
ELEVENTH Loss and sorrow caused by friends and acquaintances.
TWELFTH Much secret enmity, sorrow and privation.

*The Six of Spades*
the Six of Spades denotes a lack of opportunity and brings many hindrances to progress in those affairs governed by the House in which it falls.

*The Five of Spades*
This card denotes disputes, quarrels and importunate dealings with other people, depending upon the house in which it is placed.

*The Four of Spades*
this card has the same influence as the Eight – but in a lesser degree and relates to short journeys.

*The Three of Spades*
This card, although always a 'time' card, is very indefinite here and carries the connotation of doubt as to the ultimate result of any matter governed by the House in which it falls.

*The Two of Spades*
Not a powerful card – the Two of Spades means simply 'sorrow and tears' in whichever House it is placed–but in the Fourth House – it means sudden change and removal.

*The Ace of Spades in the Twelve Houses*
This card when pointing upwards denotes a new but difficult beginning – or important papers signed in a high building. When pointing downwards it means death, illness or bereavement. In the Third House the death of a sister – the Fourth House – a parent – the Fifth – a child and the Seventh a marital partner.

## THE CARD HOROSCOPE

Shuffle the pack of playing cards and cut the pack once with the left hand into two sections. Shuffle each section and put together again – then deal out thirteen cards in the order as illustrated in Fig 1.

```
            10
         11     9
      12           8
   1     Key card     7
      2            6
         3      5
            4
```

This is the Horoscope spread. The twelve cards represent the twelve houses of the Horoscope. The 'key' or centre card has a significance which is dealt with later.

### THE HOUSES – WHAT THEY RULE

FIRST Signifies the Enquirer -his physical appearance – general health, conditions, disposition and personaility – and if a court card is found hers – person close to him or her.

SECOND Money and possession – values – the financial prospects.
THIRD Brothers and sisters. Educational abilities, short journeys – communications.
FOURTH Parents, early home life – old age – work and home premises.
FIFTH Pleasure and amusements, offspring, love affairs – speculation.
SIXTH Work-service and enterprises, sickness, hospitals, health – employers and subordinates.
SEVENTH Marriage, relationships, partnerships – working with another.
EIGHTH Mystical experiences – birth and death – sex – shared money – wills and legacies.
NINTH Religious, philosophical, scientific or occult leanings – travel (long distance), foreigners. The countryside – the law – academic studies.
TENTH Profession, career, ambition, honour and status – public reputation – the father.
ELEVENTH Friends, hopes and wishes, hobbies, clubs, mental pursuits.
TWELFTH Inner self – service for society. Sadness and disappointments – psyche – inner life.

As in Astrology the twelve Houses are divided into two groups:

## 1 THE TRIANGLES

The 1st – 5th & 9th constitute the Life triangle.
The 10th – 2nd & 6th constitute the Material triangle.
The 7th – 11th & 3rd constitute the Relative triangle.
The 4th – 8th & 12th constitute the Terminal triangle.

## 2 THE SQUARES

The 1st – 10th & 7th & 4th The Square of Progress (as mentioned).
The 2nd – 11th & 8th & 5th The Square of Action.
The 3rd – 6th & 9th & 12th The Square of Silence.

*Some Rules for Reading a Card Horoscope*
Although, when placed in the Houses, each card can be taken almost literally, a good deal has to be left to the Reader's own intuition – but here are some *Rules to Remember*.

Hearts and Clubs are beneficial.
Diamonds are variable.
Spades usually bring troubles.

If a male Enquirer has the King of a suit in the First House – a female, the Queen or a young person the Jack – these become their significator and wield considerable influence over the Horoscope.

If a minor suit card is found in the First House, but a court card of the same suit is also present – and corresponding to the Enquirer – then the court card becomes the significator. (The rising suit or card is the card found in the First House).

Should the centre card and that in the First House be of the same suit – then that suit assumes prime importance in the Horoscope.

The personality and character of the Enquirer is always portrayed by the card in the First House and will correspond to one of the Twelve Zodiacal Signs – e.g. if the King or 4 of Spades is in the First House, the nature and disposition will be that of Cancer.

If the Queen or the 2 of Clubs is in the First House the nature and disposition will be that of Aquarius.

If the First House contains the 7 of Hearts the disposition will be a combination of Aries and Leo (see the second decanate of Aries).

The 10 of Hearts gives a combination of Aries and Sagittarius.

As the second decanate of a sign corresponds to the Fifth House and the third decanate corresponds to the Ninth House, when a second decanate card falls in the First House the card in the Fifth House has a contributory influence on his character. When a third decanate card is found in the First House (or is the rising card) as it corresponds with the Ninth House – the card in that house has an influence on the Enquirer's character.

*The First Step*

Take out all cards relating to the First House in accordance with these rules (see next Chapter).

*The Second Step*

Look at the Ruler of the Horoscope (the Rising Card) or Significator and from its position in the House judge the general prospects and circumstances of the Enquirer.

If the Enquirer is male and Hearts are in the First House and the King of Hearts is in the Horoscope its position will show his material and financial condition. If the King is absent, use either the four, seven or two of Hearts as the Diviner. Should none of these cards be present then whatever card is in the First House must be used as an indicator.

*The Third Step*

In judging the character and mental ability of the Enquirer – remember these rules.

(1) The more cards there are of the same suit – the stronger their significance in their own sphere of influence (e.g. Hearts rule pleasure, beauty, love and domestic happiness).

(2) A Spade in the centre position will predominate over all others despite the fact that all suits may be represented.

(3) Should the centre card be from onc of the other suits – particularly Clubs – even though Spades predominate in the spread – their effect will be minimised.

As so many variations occur, a lot will depend upon the judgement of the Reader.

(4) The most powerful reading occurs when the First: Fourth: Seventh and Tenth. (This is known as the Square of Progress) are occupied by the same suit cards. In this case – the centre card does not have to be of the same suit – so powerful is the meaning. Therefore – if a King of Hearts lies in the centre and the Square of Progress (of the Individual) is entirely occupied by Spades, the Enquirer would certainly be facing a major crisis in his or her life.

(5) The centre card – or Significator is very important – and wherever other cards of the same suit as the Significator fall in the Horoscope – those cards will have added force in the reading. Should the centre card be the Enquirer's actual Significator in sex and colouring. (e.g. Queen of Diamonds represents a light eyed very fair skinned woman with blonde, red or snow white hair) then the most significant cards in the Horoscope will be Diamonds.

When you have considered these points, you must turn your attention to the character and mentality of the Enquirer.

*Point 1* The King represents the individual character. The Enquirer's character is always judged from the King of the same suit as the card in House 1 (the Rising Card) or if it is not present – from one of the cards of that suit allied to the King.

*Point 2* The Queen represents the individual personality. The Enquirer's personality is always judged from the Queen of the same suit as the Rising Card (that in House 1) or from one of the three suit cards allied to the Queen.

*Point 3* The Jack represents the mentality. The Enquirer's mentality is judged from the Jack of the suit which is Rising (in House 1) on one of his allied cards.

These three matters will be judged according to the position of these cards in the houses of the Card Horoscope, and if the Reader does not possess a basic knowledge of Astrology, the intuition will have to be used.

*As an Example of the Above*

If a Heart is in the First House (or is the Rising Card) and the King of Hearts or one of the three cards allied to him is found in the Eleventh House – this would denote a very friendly, convivial, sociable person, possessing strong ambition, broad-minded, with a love of friends and interested in reform.

The personality would be under the rule of the Queen of Hearts and should the Queen or any of her three allied cards be present in the Fifth House – it would show a person with a love of pleasure, children, a talent for singing or in the fine Arts and sincere affections.

The mental characteristics – ruled by the Knave of Hearts or his three allied cards – particularly if placed in the Third House – would denote a studious, quick mind, with a love of travel, variety and change and a love of literature.

Each suit, having its own interpretation, must also be taken into consideration – and the Knave of Spades would have an entirely different mentality to the Knave of Hearts. The temperament may also be determined from the number of cards of each suit in the Card Horoscope:

Hearts predominating denote an open fiery temperament;

Diamonds predominating denote a highly strung but earthy temperament;

Clubs predominating denote a calm, sanguine philosophic temperament;

Spades predominating denote a watery, secret, subtle temperament.

*The Card Horoscope Reading*

Step 1 Shuffle the pack. The Enquirer cuts it into three sections which are combined and then fanned across the table. The Enquirer chooses 12 cards at random which will be placed in the House positions (see Fig. 1.) This procedure is repeated but this time the Enquirer chooses only one card – the Key Card or Significator which is placed in the middle (see Fig.2.) Commence

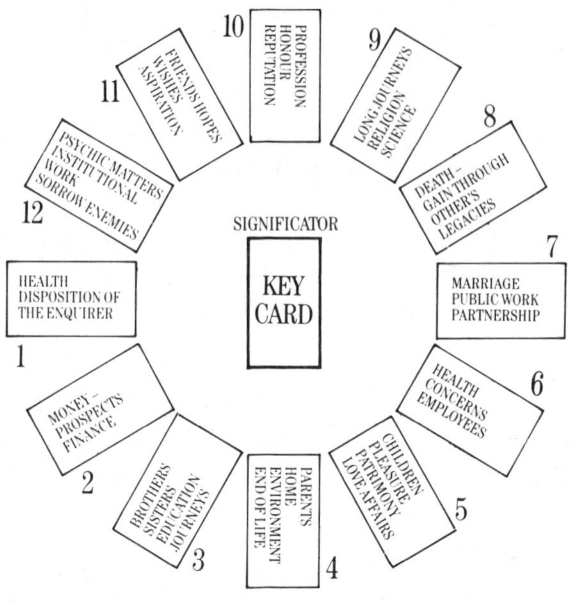


*Fig.1*

your reading from the First House. When the First House has been dealt with thoroughly, interpret the other cards according to their placement in the House always keeping in mind the significance of the Centre or Key Card, particularly if it is of the same suit as those being read. Do not forget to assess the relative importance of the suits and to find whether one is significantly predominant.

The difference between an ordinary card spread or reading and the Astrological Map lies in the latter's comprehensiveness. The Houses cover every aspect of the Enquirer's life. Because of this broad canvas, accurate interpretation relies more on intuitional judgement than a detailed knowledge of Astrology, although the latter is an advantage.

*Fig.2.*

*Example of a Horoscope*

The study of the First House – giving the Enquirer's nature, personality and mentality.

The diagram shows the 5 of Diamonds as the Rising Card – (in the First House). The Suit of Clubs (as one is also in the centre) is the predominant suit (particularly with the key card or significator being Clubs) – it denotes a keen intellect, and good business sense combining to bring success to the Enquirer.

The King of Diamonds is also in the map – so this card becomes the ruler of the map and Significator of the Reader. It describes a man (usually fair – but the colouring is not so important) kind, loving, sometimes unpredictable – connected with financial concerns, banking and stock market. The 5 of Diamonds will bring financial rewards and material benefit and – most important – general good health. As it corresponds to the sign of Tarus – and also with the second decanate of that sign – the general nature or attitude of the Enquirer will be Taurean – with Virgoan influences. The second decanate also corresponds with the 5th House which is occupied by the King of Diamonds – showing this card to be of prime importance in the map. The 2 of Diamonds – the only other card in this suit – is in 12th house. This means the Reader's concerns may be secret – but it is more likely to mean he gains from undertakings connected with large institutions (e.g. hospitals).

The individual character – having the King of Diamonds in the map and a card of the same suit in the First House – will come under Capricorn – so the Reader is ambitious, enterprising, economical – a leader determined to achieve status and position.

The 5 and 2 of Diamonds – allied to the Queen – represents a consistent, stable, determined personality, kind, affectionate, possessing taste and discrimination, a good memory, but inclined to being obstinate and critical.

None of the cards connected with the Knave of Diamonds – or the Knave is present. The clue to the Enquirer's mentality is found in the 3rd House which contains 7 of Clubs – ruled by Libra – and denoting a well balanced intuitive mind of an imitative and artistic bent.

The 4 of Hearts and 4 of Clubs present in the map give a fiery sanguine nature strong both emotionally and intellectually.

Having dealt with the Enquirer himself now the cards in the other Eleven Houses must be read.

THE SECOND HOUSE The 4 of Hearts brings success in money matters generally and gain through social matters and other people.

THE THIRD HOUSE The 7 of Clubs here could either mean recognition or reward comes at the end of a short journey – rewards and prestige through educational matters – or rewards or awards to a brother or sister.

THE FOURTH HOUSE The Queen of Hearts denotes the Enquirer has had a happy stable home life – an affectionate mother.

THE FIFTH HOUSE The King of Diamonds here means successful male progeny – but as this card also signifies the Enquirer – it also can denote that the Enquirer is in danger of becoming addicted to gambling or takes too many risks.

THE SIXTH HOUSE This card denotes pleasure – good health and reliable workers or subordinates.

THE SEVENTH HOUSE The 4 of Clubs here – for a male Enquirer signifies an affectionate, loyal, artistic, talented wife who will be a good mother. It also denotes success in professional partnership – public gain and business or employment expansion through travel.

THE EIGHTH HOUSE The Ace of Clubs is most meaningful here – denoting gain through marriage (being of the same suit as the card in the marriage house (7th)) It also denotes benefits from wills, or legacies and means the Enquirer will at some time be much involved with legal documents or business deeds.

THE NINTH HOUSE Having the 6 of Hearts here – means that courtship and marriage could in some way be connected with travel and foreign countries. It is also beneficial in the sphere of foreign residence and long journeys. As the Queen of the same suit is in the Fourth House – it could also mean a happy retirement overseas.

THE TENTH HOUSE Luckily the 4 of Spades has little significance here – being the only one of its suit in the map – and only accentuates the benefits of travel in the Enquirer's profession or career.

THE ELEVENTH HOUSE The 9 of Clubs is a very good card to have – particularly here. It means that friends will greatly help the Enquirer's business or profession.

THE TWELFTH HOUSE The 2 of Diamonds here denotes a secret matter which will bring unexpected gain. It also can mean the Enquirer has some past connection with an institution, which was beneficial.

## THE SIGNIFICATOR – OR KEY CARD

*The Six of Clubs*
Because of the other three Clubs in the horoscope map – this card becomes very important and will have great influence, on the future of the Enquirer.

It is a very propitious card – meaning that the Enquirer, at some time, will be offered a very important post – a business offer – a responsible position that will bring promotions honour and eventual success in his chosen career.

*Chapter Nine*

# Some Advice on Reading the Tarot Cards

At the two Sydney universities where I taught tarot for the Students Union, I suggested my pupils buy large sticky labels for the backs of the cards, and that they write the meanings of each card on them. There are often four or five differing meanings and each card is affected by those nearest to it. As there are 78 tarot cards, there are too many meanings to commit to memory at first, and sometimes one of the subsidiary meanings applies, not the main, traditional interpretation.

Interpretation i.e. stringing the meanings together to form a pattern only comes easily with practice. I always give three or four 'spreads' of the cards to make sure I am not reading my client's mind and telling them what they want to hear, which often does occur in the first reading of the cards.

Reversals were only introduced in the late 19th century as they are negative in nature and I do not use them as I believe enough negative cards are contained in the pack to give two sides to every issue.

I have told pupils they must learn the meanings, as in the rules of grammar, before they can take liberties with the interpretation. The cards serve as a guide or trigger to the intuition, and each reader eventually uses meanings peculiar to themselves. It is as dangerous to encourage someone to act beyond his or her capacities as it is to instil fear and self doubt into the person you are reading for. The message of the cards themselves tends to be exaggerated because of their usual impact so I am always careful not to 'go over the top' in a reading.

As an example, I read for a girl who had had many chances of marriage but had let them all go by because a clairvoyant had told her she should marry a millionaire. I saw a moderately wealthy man coming into her life but had to tell her she would only find unhappiness if she persisted in valuing the money more than the man.

The Death card which frightens so many more often means a transformation, not death. There are Swords cards in the tarot pack and Spades in the playing pack denoting loss, grief, darkness and despair which, to me, frequently bring a sense of bereavement.

Always strive to be honest, tactful and positive. If the spreads I lay out do not reveal the Strength card I may omit certain information i.e. I may foretell a serious illness instead of death because, in my opinion, the client would worry and be unable to cope with such knowledge. Only if the client is middle-aged or older and strength appears early in the spread am I able to give all the information, and on those occasions, I dwell more on the positive happenings. If my client does not go away happier than they were prior to my reading, I have not done my task properly.

In my family of five generations of 'see – ers' there has always been the tradition of refusing to read the cards of anyone under 21. My own two sons had to wait until they attained their majority for my mother to give them a reading. I think it is wise practice. Reading for susceptible sensitive adolescents could be harmful and dangerous.

When a couple are truly united in spirit, the cards will mirror their mutual concerns (and many mothers are so concerned with their children, their own affairs are sometimes only glossed over in a reading). I do not read such couples separately. If they both come to see me I divide the spreads between them. This need not apply to the tarot cards as they sometimes give different psychological insights into their individual characters. For colourings of the court cards, always look at the skin first, then eyes, then hair. Green eyes will turn a 'Heart' person (brown hair and fair skin) into a 'Club' (usually hazel or green eyes, light olive skin and mid-brown hair). Grey or white hair will lighten the client's original colour so that 'Spades' (the Latin type) becomes 'Clubs', 'Clubs' becomes 'Hearts', and 'Hearts' becomes 'Diamonds'.

When reading for clients from a dark skinned race, the traditional colouring classification may not apply as sometimes their lover, family and friends are classed as 'Spades'. As the King, Queen and Jack of Spades have important secondary meanings, and all Spades court cards denote foreign shores or concerns, it is better to dispense with the rules and rely on your intuition to describe people who appear in the reading.

The Age rule in the tarot, the Knave, denotes girl or boy under 21, the Knight a man of 21 – 35 years, and the King a man of 35 years or over. The Queen is a woman of any age. In the playing cards the Jack denotes a young man and the King an older man, but sometimes people appear older or younger because of their attitude to life i.e. an older man may be a 'Peter Pan' and often comes up next to the Fool (the rebellious, non-materialistic dreamer) and a younger man is shown next to the Hermit (the wise, deliberate, prudent traveller through life).

If the Fool appears in a central position, to me it denotes a non-materialistic nature, and if the strength card appears, I know that even if the client seems outwardly to be weak, vaccilating, over emotional or impractical, he or she is capable of self honesty and has an inner strength (albeit untapped) which will bolster and protect them all their lives. These are the 'old souls'. Strength lessens all negativity in a reading.

When reading I use two packs of tarot cards. One pack is my personal pack which I shuffle, visualising a bridge stretching between the client and myself and I then ask the client to cut the pack into three sections. The top cards of these having been noted, I then reassemble the pack and proceed to give two or three 'spreads' to make sure the same pattern is recurring. Then I ask the client to shuffle the second pack and lay out two more spreads to make sure.

# List of Books

*The Book of Tarot* by Susan Gerulskis-Estes
*The Tarot* by Alfred Douglas
*Tarotmania* by Jan Woudhuysen
*Tarot Cards For Fun And Fortune Telling* by Stuart R. Kaplan
*The Pictorial Key to the Tarot* by A. E. White